90 Days of Encouragement

These daily meditations are designed to encourage first responders in their faith when life seems to be out of control

by

International Board Members
of
FCFInternational

Fellowship of Christian Firefighters International

Preface

The fire service can be a difficult place to serve in for Christian first responders. Daily we are bombarded with images and events that test our faith to the very core. Firefighters can take comfort and gain encouragement from the truth contained within the Bible and from others in the fire service who have walked down similar roads.

Christianity is more than a religious system that first responders must keep in order to please God. Christianity is a relationship with a creator God who loves us and dispatched His Son Jesus Christ to pay the penalty for the bad things we have done in life (John 3:16). Almost every first responder will admit that they have sinned against God (Romans 3:23). Some will even have knowledge in the fact that there is a penalty for those sins (Romans 6:23). For those first responders who confess their sins and believe on the Lord Jesus Christ as their Savior will inherit eternal life (Romans 10:9).

Once we have begun our relationship with God it is important for us to strengthen and grow that relationship. In the fire service we are used to training in order to improve our skills and abilities. We watch videos, take on-line classes, and even travel in order to be proficient in our roles as first responders. If we are willing to go the extra mile in our roles as firefighters, why do some Christian first responders choose not to grow in their faith? The same technology available for training firefighters is available to learning more about Christ.

The Fellowship of Christian Firefighters International is here to encourage first responders in their faith. Our desire is to provide resources that not only help you to grow but help you to thrive in the department God has called you to.

Meet the Authors

Keith Helms - Keith Helms is a retired firefighter. He was a member of the Charlotte Fire Department for 29 years. He and his wife, Jane, have 3 grown children and 4 grandchildren. Keith believed in Jesus Christ as his savior in January of 1980. Early in his relationship with the Lord, Keith was introduced to the ministry of discipleship. His desire to minister in the fire service continues to be focused on discipling others.

Wayne Detzler - Straight after finishing his ministry training at Wheaton Graduate School Wayne, Margaret, and their infant daughter set off for missionary service. Their first assignment was in Germany, where Wayne learned to preach in the atmosphere of a region-wide awakening. Later their son, Mark, was born in Germany before they left for England. For thirteen years they served churches in England, where Wayne also developed a ministry among British police.

In 1983 Wayne and Margaret returned to the United States, where Wayne combined teaching and pastoral ministries. While living in Meriden, CT Wayne became chaplain of the Meriden Fire Department in 1988. He helped to launch a chapter of FCFI. In 1994 he moved to Charlotte, NC where he became chaplain of the Charlotte Fire Department and an active FCFI member. In 2007 he entered his present assignment as chaplain of the Long Hill Fire Department in Trumbull, CT.

The driving force in Wayne's life is making disciples. He takes Matt. 28:19 as a life ministry. Wherever they live, Wayne seeks for guys to disciple. Whether teaching at a local university or meeting with firefighters, he is always looking for F-A-T fellows. These are people who are Faithful, Available, and Teachable. When Wayne finds them, he meets with them to lead them deeper into the Christian life.

Rob Hitt - Rob was born and raised in Greenville, S.C. and born again through the Lord Jesus Christ when he was 17, in 1983. That same year, Rob entered the fire service, with his new faith. Rob's interest in the fire service was through his grandfather Heyward Hitt. After high school, he studied criminal justice but the Lord had other plans for him when he called him into the fire service. Rob married his wonderful wife Debbie, in 1993, served 9 years in the S.C. Army National Guard, as a 91 Bravo Combat Medic. Together Rob and his wife had 5 beautiful children, one who is planning to be a missionary to Holland. Rob presently works at the Duncan Chapel Fire Department in Greenville, S.C. Rob became a member of the Fellowship of Christian Firefighters, in the mid-80's and served as the S.C. Regional Director and now serves on the International Board. To sum up, his Christian life, Rob has been blessed by the Lord who has given him the ability to obtain, perform and minister for His Kingdom. Rob loves to say as the Apostle Paul, "I am what I am, by the grace of God."

Craig Duck – Craig Duck is a retired lieutenant from the District of Columbia Fire Department who continues to serve his community as a volunteer firefighter in Boydton, Virginia. He and his wife, Holly, have 4 grown children. After receiving Jesus Christ as his Lord and Savior, Craig, has worked hard to glorify God in the fire service. Craig currently serves as your President/Missionary.

Bracket Christians – Day 1
By Craig Duck – President/Missionary

Read II Thessalonians 2:13-17

Encouragement for the day – *"So then, brothers and sisters, stand firm and hold fast to the teachings we passed on to you, whether by word of mouth or by letter."*
2 Thessalonians 2:15 NIV

Whenever we get a new fire truck in the District of Columbia it is a big deal. The factory technicians will come out for several days and teach us how to operate and drive it. The apparatus division will give us all new tools and brackets to hold them in place. The captain of the company will assign each shift tasks to complete and the drivers will choose where to place all of the mounting brackets. The mounting brackets are important because they hold the tools firmly in place until needed. If the apparatus didn't have brackets than the tools would slide all over the place and become damaged or not easy to locate. Once all of the tools are mounted the apparatus can go in service and respond on emergencies.

Life can be difficult for Christian first responders. There are people and situations that try and pull you away from Biblical principles. Christian first responders that are not fully grounded in those Biblical principles are like tools stuffed in a compartment with no brackets. When the driver makes a quick turn, all of the tools will slide to the other side of the compartment and potentially become useless. Paul encouraged the believers in the Thessalonian church to hold fast to the teachings they have received. The Word of God can be our bracket, holding us firmly in place, if we daily read what it says and apply it to our lives in the fire service. So let's commit to obeying what God has instructed us to do and to hold on to it as tight as our brackets hold on to our tools.

Lord, thank you for the Bible. Help me to hold fast to what You have taught me.

Encouragement is everyone's priority!!

Notes

_____

_____

_____

_____

_____

_____

_____

_____

_____

_____

_____

Acknowledging Jesus – Day 2
By Wayne Detzler – International Board Member

Read I John 4:1-20

"If anyone acknowledges that Jesus is the Son of God, God lives in them and they in God. And so we know and rely on the love God has for us."

1 John 4:15-16 NIV

This ringing assurance of God's love strengthens me every day. Several years ago I memorized First John with my friend, Bill Ginter in Meriden, CT. Each time I review these verses, my reliance on God's love is strengthened. We visited the International Church in Beijing one Sunday. To my great delight the preacher chose these words as his text: "We know and rely on the love God has for us."

How can Christian First Responders acknowledge Jesus around the station? _____
_____
.

What are some appropriate ways to share your faith on emergencies? _____
_____
.

List several ways to show love to other first responders: __
_____

Retirement – Day 3
By Keith Helms – International Board Member

Read II Timothy

Ever since I retired in Dec. 2010, the most frequent question that I am asked by firefighters is "How is retirement?" My typical response is that it is great. For most people in today's society, a great retirement implies that you are free of all worries. Every day is like an all-inclusive cruise to the Caribbean. You don't "have to" do anything. My retirement is not like that. While I don't have a lot of "have to's", there is a daily list of "want to's". I want to be more faithful in my study of God's Word. I want to be more focused on prayer and my communion with God the Father, God the Son, and God the Holy Spirit. I want my walk with Christ to be evidenced in how I treat my wife, my children, my grandchildren, and others. I want to be fully engaged in the spiritual battle that surrounds us. I have retired from the Charlotte fire Department. I have not retired from my service for Christ.

A good friend of mine who was approaching retirement once said that he was going to keep rowing until he got to the other side. The meaning was that he wanted to continue working diligently until he retired. He didn't want to take his oars out of the water and coast the last months of his career. That is how we should look at retirement in this life. While we may be retired from a career, we should never retire from serving Christ and others. Keep your oars in the water. You haven't reached the other side yet.

"I have fought the good fight, I have finished the race, I have kept the faith." 2 Timothy 4:7

A Godly Heritage – Day 4
By Craig Duck – President/Missionary FCFInternational

Read II John

Encouragement for the day – *"It has given me great joy to find some of your children walking in the truth, just as the Father commanded us"*

II John 4 NIV

I remember a time when I was an instructor at the training academy. As I was looking over the names of the new recruits, one name jumped out at me. I had recognized the name of a son of one of the firefighters I have worked with before. As the weeks progressed the recruits were doing remarkably well. That graduation ceremony was one of the best I ever attended. This recruit's father was allowed to hand him his diploma. I will never forget how proud that firefighter was of his son and all of the accomplishments he had made during the training academy. He was truly filled with great joy over the event.

John, in today's Bible verse, is also filled with joy. John is writing this letter, II John, to an "elect lady and her children". We read that John is rejoicing in the fact that this lady and her children are walking in truth. As first responders we can easily say that our children are one of our greatest joys. Just sit and listen as folks at the station talk about what their children are doing. My prayer is that my children will walk with God all of their life. My hope is that they will daily read their Bibles, always be found serving in a Bible believing church, and constantly striving to follow God's principles. I hope that this is your prayer for your children as well. Together we can have "great joy to find" our "children walking in the truth".

Lord, thank you for the children You have given me. Help me to spend time with them each day.

Have you heard? Encouragement is contagious!!

Notes

_____

_____

_____

_____

_____

_____

_____

_____

_____

_____

For Such a Time as This – Day 5

By Wayne Detzler – International Board Member

Read Esther Chapter 4

"For such a time as this" This morning I am reading the story of Esther, the courageous queen. When Mordecai, her cousin, challenges her to speak up on behalf of her own Jewish people he says: "Who knows but what you have come to royal position for such a time as this?" (Esther 4:14 NIV) The amazing truth is this: Each of us is part of God's plan. God has a special purpose for each of our lives, and we find great delight when we fulfill that purpose. This powerful truth is echoed by the Apostle Paul: "And we know that in all things God works for the good of those who love him, who have been called according to his purpose." (Romans 8:28 NIV)

In what ways do you believe God has placed you in your department at this specific time? _____

_____

How can we fulfill God's plan in the fire service? _____

_____

A Better Hope – Day 6

By Keith Helms – International Board Member

Heb. 7:19 – *"(for the law made nothing perfect); but on the other hand, a better hope is introduced, through which we draw near to God."*

Hebrews 7:19 ESV

What are the common hopes of firefighters? A promotion…a transfer to a busy company…a good working fire…a spouse that greets you affectionately when you get home…a new truck? Most of our hopes are built on the foundation of a desire for a better life now. While God can provide for our current comfort, that should not be the centrality of a believer's hope. Hebrews 7:19 states that God offers a better hope through which we can draw near to Him. The Lord offers a relationship with Him over momentary comfort. You can pray for less stress in your day and God may or may not provide relief. Pray and seek intimacy with Him and He will allow you to be drawn to Him. That is a better hope.

For further study, begin with Ps. 73:78; Romans 7:4-6; Galatians 2-3

Making Adjustments – Day 7

By Craig Duck – President/Missionary FCFInternational

Read Hebrews 11:30 – 12:1

Encouragement for the day – *"Therefore, since we are surrounded by so great a cloud of witnesses, let us also lay aside every weight, and sin which clings so closely, and let us run with endurance the race that is set before us, looking to Jesus, the founder and perfecter of our faith, who for the joy that was set before him endured the cross, despising the shame, and is seated at the right hand of the throne of God."*

Hebrews 12:1-2 ESV

In the fire service we are constantly making adjustments. An incident commander is listening to all of the reports from company officers about the conditions inside the building. When conditions deteriorate to a point where the incident commander is not comfortable he/she will make an adjustment from an interior to an exterior attack. As a company officer I have been on fires where we have come up short with hose or have gone the wrong direction. It is our job as a company to make the proper adjustments in order to put the fire out. First responders will even have to make adjustments when the equipment they are utilizing is not working properly. Making adjustments allows us to accomplish our goal of handling the emergency and returning the situation back to a level of normalcy.

The Bible is constantly encouraging us to evaluate what we are doing in light of God's word the Bible and make adjustments to our life accordingly. As a Christian first responder it is easy for us to fall into various kinds of sin, and that never pleases God. Read the roll of honor of the heroes of the faith in Hebrews chapter 11 and you will be reminded of all the normal everyday people who did extra ordinary things for God. The writer of Hebrews reminds us that we can be just like them if we evaluate our lives and readjust them as needed. I love the analogy of sin to weight. We wouldn't want to run a race with our fire gear on, why would we want to live life with so much sin? I urge all of us to confess our sins to God and make those adjustments for the glory of God.

Lord, thank you that I am able to confess my sins to You and You will forgive them.

Everyone needs encouragement sometime!!

God Never Changes – Day 8

By Wayne Detzler – International Board Member

Read James 1:12-18

"Whatever is good and perfect comes down to us from God our Father, who created all the lights in the heavens. He never changes or casts a shifting shadow."
James 1:17 NLT

James reminds us that every good thing we have comes from God. He is the source of all that is right in our lives. Then James adds the note that there is no variance with God. He always keeps on giving. This is an age-old truth. It is King David himself who framed this phrase when writing the psalms: "I said to the LORD, "You are my Master! Every good thing I have comes from you." (Psalm 16:2 NLT)

What good things has God blessed you with this past year? _____

_____

In what ways have you observed that God never changes?

_____

_____

Who is Andrew? – Day 9

By Keith Helms – International Board Member

How would you like to always be known as someone's brother? In each of the four gospels, Andrew is referred to as Simon Peter's brother. In fact, he is seldom mentioned by name in the New Testament. Andrew was one of the 12 Apostles, yet we know very little about him. Here is what we do know:

- He was a fisherman with his brother (Matt.4:18; Mark 1:16).
- They were from the town of Bethsaida (John 1:44).
- Before he saw Jesus, Andrew was a disciple of John the Baptist (John 1:40).
- Tradition holds that Andrew died on a cross at Patrae, in Achaia, a Grecian Colony.

That is basically all that we know about Andrew. Every other detail about him is unknown, with one exception. Andrew had one unique characteristic. He was so concerned about others that he was passionate about bringing others to Jesus. When Andrew first saw Jesus, he left John the Baptist and began to follow Jesus. After hearing the Lord talk, he went to his brother, Peter, telling him that they had found the Messiah (the Christ) and he brought Peter to Jesus. When the 5000 needed to be fed and the other disciples wanted to send everyone away to fend for themselves, Andrew found a young boy who had 5 loaves of bread and 2 fish. He brought the boy to Jesus who miraculously fed all of the 5000 (John 6:1-14). When Andrew was told about some Greek men who wanted to see Jesus, Andrew took their request to Jesus (John 12:22).

Andrew apparently had one dominating passion...the Lord Jesus Christ. It is possible that as an earlier disciple of John the Baptist, Andrew had learned one of John's teachings. In John 3:30, John said, "He (Christ) must increase, but I must decrease." We don't know if Andrew was bothered by the fact that he lived in his brother's shadow. We do know that nothing prevented him from bringing people and their concerns to Christ. While he may not have received much recognition, Andrew knew that his brother, the 5000, and the Greek men needed Jesus. He wanted Christ to be glorified. What motivated Andrew? Apparently it was not fame or the applause of others. His motivation should be our motivation. We should have an overwhelming desire to bring others to Christ and to glorify Him. When did you last bring someone to the Savior?

Piercing Nozzles – Day 10

By Craig Duck – President/Missionary FCFInternational

Read Hebrews 4:11-13

Encouragement for the day – *"For the word of God is living and active, sharper than any two-edged sword, piercing to the division of soul and of spirit, of joints and of marrow, and discerning the thoughts and intentions of the heart."*

Hebrews 4:12 ESV

Piercing nozzles are relatively new in the fire service. I first saw them used for car fires. It is always difficult to get the hoods opened up after the cable burns off. More than several times we would fight to open the hood enough to get the fire extinguished. Over the years someone developed a nozzle that would pierce the metal hood and apply the extinguishing agent directly to the fire. Recently, I saw this idea developed into a bigger product capable of piercing concrete buildings. This new tool is designed to go on the end of an aerial ladder and once the building exterior has been pierced the real work of extinguishing the fire can begin.

In Hebrews 4:12 we learn that the Bible is capable of extinguishing the flames of our sin and rebellion. The Bible is alive because God brought it into existence. The

Bible is also considered alive because it is able to change people's lives. Through the work of the Holy Spirit we learn of what pleases God and what does not. As we read the Bible we can easily become convicted of our sin, it is as if God Himself were talking directly to us. In the fire service we build up many walls to protect us. The Bible is able to pierce those walls just like a piercing nozzle and get to the heart of the matter. Through regular study of God's word we are able to find those things that displease God and correct them. Then our very thoughts and actions can begin to mirror Jesus Christ and we will see real change within the fire service.

Lord, help me to study the Bible every day and learn how to please You.

Encouragement goes a long way when shared with a friend!!

Notes

_____

_____

_____

_____

_____

_____

Meeting Jesus – Day 11

By Wayne Detzler – International Board Member

"But I know this: I was blind, and now I can see!"

John 9:25 NLT

All his life the man had seen nothing. Then he met Jesus, and Jesus healed his blindness. The man's testimony is as clear as his newly acquired vision. This is a very personal meaning to the statement of Jesus: "I am the light of the world." (John 9:5 NLT) When the man met Jesus, his whole life changed. Many years ago we were in a chapel service at Wheaton College when a student cried out. It turned out that she had been virtually blind, but during that rather routine worship experience Jesus healed her. After we meet Jesus, nothing is ever the same.

How did you meet Jesus? _____

_____

How has your life been different? _____

_____

When was the last time you shared Jesus with someone?

_____

_____

The Proud Man – Day 12

By Keith Helms – International Board Member

Read Proverbs Chapter 18

The foundational message from the proud person is that life can work without trust in God. Listen to the words of Jonathan Edwards, "This (pride) is the main door by which the devil comes into the hearts of those who are zealous for the advancement of Christ. It is the chief inlet of smoke from the bottomless pit to darken the mind and mislead the judgment, and the main handle by which Satan takes hold of Christians to hinder a work of God."

The Bible specifically mentions pride as a sin that God hates (Prov. 8:13; Prov. 16:5; 1 Peter 5:5-6). God is a jealous God; He hates anything that is intended to rob Him of His glory (Ex. 20:5; Ex. 34:14; Ezek. 39:25). The sole aim of pride is to glorify self above glorifying God. The proud person may exhibit a grand showing of his religious efforts to glorify God, but underneath his actions exists a primary desire to make life work without trusting in God. Make no mistake about it, God will never cooperate with or tolerate any desire or plan that exists for the primary goal of self-glorification. As is true for all sin, Christ died so that the sin of pride could be forgiven.

What are we to do about pride? Are we to increase our efforts to fight against it? Are there ways or steps that we can follow that will give us victory over pride? While there are most definitely spiritual disciplines that will facilitate our battles with the flesh, they are not the basis of our battle. If we are to engage in the battle within our heart, we must acknowledge our impotency and we must rely on the Holy Spirit. Sins of the flesh, including pride, cannot be managed through self-effort. Without reliance on the Holy Spirit, all of our well-intended efforts are analogous to attempts of someone on the Titanic trying to keep the chairs in line. It may look good for a while, but the ship is sinking. Self-efforts may similarly look good, but there is no victory over sin without the Holy Spirit (Romans 8:12-17; Gal. 5:16-25). Walking with the Spirit leads to confession, brokenness, repentance, and revival. It is a cycle that moves us along the path of spiritual maturity and relational holiness.

Notes

_____

_____

_____

_____

_____

_____

Company Pride – Day 13

By Craig Duck – President/Missionary FCFInternational

Read Romans 12:1-8

Encouragement for the day – *"For I say, through the grace given me, to everyone who is among you, not to think of himself more highly than he ought to think, but to think soberly, as God has dealt to each one a measure of faith."*

Romans 12:3 NKJV

The fire service can be a place where people boast a lot. Since the early days of the fire service, company pride has always been instilled upon members. I love reading the history books and learning of company names like Vigilant Hose Company, Perseverance Hose Company 5, Independence Hose Company 3, and many more. In Washington, DC one can go into most firehouses and soon a discussion will begin about how great their company is and why. One has to be careful in the fire service about boasting too much. We have all come across first responders who think that fires would still be burning out of control if they weren't there. On the fireground it takes everybody efficiently and quickly accomplishing their task for the fire to go out.

In Romans, Paul warns us to be careful about boasting great things. He reminds us that God has given each of us unique abilities and talents. When we understand that principle, and efficiently work together for good, God can use our team to accomplish great things for His glory. When we chose to not use our God given abilities alongside other Christian firefighters we begin to become prideful, thinking we are better than everyone else. God doesn't use just one person in ministry, he uses a team of committed people to accomplish His will. When I was assigned to a busy company in Columbia Heights we used to tell everyone to "leave their feelings at the door". Perhaps we should have had a sign that read, "Leave your prideful nature at the door". I encourage all of us to evaluate why and how we do things, making sure we do everything for the right reason.

Lord, thank you for the Bible which helps me to learn how You want me to act around the station.

Encouraging first responders by being there!!

Notes

_____

_____

Rescue Me – Day 14

By Wayne Detzler – International Board Member

"Please, God, rescue me! Come quickly, LORD, and help me."

Psalm 70:1 NLT

David launches this psalm with a cry to God. As the Psalm develops, David fills in the picture. He demonstrates the presence and power of God. Then the king's heart sings this worship song: "But may all who search for you be filled with joy and gladness in you. May those who love your salvation repeatedly shout, 'God is great!'" (Psalm 70:4 NLT) We never ever seek the Lord in vain. He is always there for those who call on Him. So, let's praise Him!

When was the last time you sang a song of worship during your daily devotions? _____

_____

Is your life filled with joy and gladness? If not Why? _____

_____

What can you change in your life in order to bring joy and gladness to others? _____

Toolbox or Tool Belt – Day 15

By Keith Helms – International Board Member

Read Ephesians Chapter 6

Firefighters often use the reference to a toolbox when talking about specific tactics and resources. After attending a training session about a firefighting concept, you may hear firefighters say that they will put that in their toolbox. The intent is that they will store the concept in their mental "toolbox" so that they can pull it out when the need arises. Examples include different types of nozzles, foam application, types of ventilation, vehicular extrication techniques, etc. The point is that although the firefighter will not be using these every day, he wants to be able to utilize the concept or resource when it will facilitate the mitigation of the incident.

When we use this same reference to our spiritual lives, we face a problem that is very prevalent today. We often hear a good sermon on a biblical discipline (Bible study, prayer, fellowship, worship) and we decide to place it in our spiritual toolbox. We confidently store it away with the thought that we will retrieve it when the need arises. Praying without ceasing, studying God's Word, encouraging one another, loving and forgiving others…we place these in our toolbox until life's problems penetrate our sense of personal comfort and wellbeing. And when the problems arise (an inevitable consequence of a fallen world), we scramble to locate our toolbox and find the appropriate tool that will numb our pain, feed our desire for comfort, and fix the problem. I can only imagine God's disdain for our foolishness. A better reference for a believer is a tool belt which is to be worn. A spiritual tool belt is to be worn at all times and can be likened to the spiritual armor as mentioned in Ephesians 6:10-18. We recently posted a picture on FaceBook of a firefighter kneeling at a fire with the caption "When life is too Hot to Stand….Kneel". While this is good advice, why not kneel at all times? Why wait until life gets difficult? Don't place your spiritual disciplines in a tool box. Keep them tightly secured to your body. Walking with Christ requires a tool belt, not a tool box.

Notes

_____

_____

_____

_____

_____

_____

Don't Touch the Third Rail – Day 16

By Craig Duck – President/Missionary FCFInternational

Read I Corinthians 6:12-20

Encouragement for the day – *"Flee sexual immorality. Every sin that a man does is outside the body, but he who commits sexual immorality sins against his own body."*

I Corinthians 6:18 NKJV

In Washington, DC we have a metro commuter train. Since I have been on the job we have been responsible as a department to respond to any emergency within the metro rail system. The DC Fire and EMS Department does a lot of training to ensure that we are prepared for emergencies within the system and that our members are safe. One of the tools that we have is a warning strobe alarm device, simply known as a WASAD. The WASAD is hooked up to the third rail when power has been confirmed down (turned off) and will alert members when the third rail has been accidently activated. The warning strobe and the alarm will sound. The obvious reason to use this device is for safety of first responders as they work in the track bed. You wouldn't want to touch the third rail in order to find out if the power is on, that is just plain stupid.

The Bible talks a lot about marriage. The institution of marriage has been set up by God (Genesis 2:23-24), is designed to be a lifelong commitment (Matthew 19:6), and men are told to love their wives (Ephesians 5:25). When a believing husband and wife commit to following God's plan for marriage it shows the world a picture of the oneness of Christ and His church. Unfortunately the world has polluted and even mocked the Biblical plan for marriage. In the fire service there are many people who will say it is ok to have sex outside of marriage. The Bible is clear that sex is reserved for marriage. It is not ok to have sex before marriage or to have sex with someone that is not your spouse when you are married. We are told in the metro rail system to never touch the third rail, always treat it as if its power is on. Likewise it would be just as foolish to touch someone who is not your spouse.

Lord, help me to remain faithful to my spouse and obedient to Your word.

Encouragement, pass it on!!

Notes

_____

_____

_____

House of Prayer – Day 17

By Wayne Detzler – International Board Member

Jesus said to them, "The Scriptures declare, 'My Temple will be called a house of prayer for all nations."

Mark 11:17 NLT

Jesus placed a primary emphasis on prayer. He kept this emphasis going throughout His ministry on earth, and now He stands at the right hand of the Father praying for us. It is no wonder, then, that the Apostle Paul struck the same chord: "I urge you, first of all, to pray for all people. Ask God to help them; intercede on their behalf, and give thanks for them." (1 Tim. 2:1 NLT) Over the past years the Lord has narrowed my ministry focus to prayer, and this has grown in the vibrant prayer atmosphere on our beloved Black Rock Church. As prayer pastor I am part of a prayer team that knows more about prayer than I will ever know. This may be what the Apostle Paul meant, when he wrote: "In every place of worship, I want men [and women] to pray with holy hands lifted up to God, free from anger and controversy." (1 Tim. 2:8 NLT)

How can you have a better, more effective prayer life? ___

_____

Prayer – Day 18

By Rob Hitt – International Board Member

BEYOND THE BORDERS ... Tonight I am on shift at the fire department. As I sit in the alarm room, the thought of prayer comes to mind. In this room, it is utilized for communication. Communication is a vital entity, for first responders at every level. Without proper communication, tragedy could result. The same holds true for Christian firefighters; without a continual, proper and routine communication with the Lord, we will become "out of range" with the Lord and miss out on great opportunities for fellowship and what He has to say to us. Let us all keep on "the right channel" of communication with the Lord daily! "Lord, help us to talk and fellowship with you on a day by day basis, so that we can have that channel open to the throne of righteousness! Amen."

How can you cultivate an active prayer life? _____

_____

When is the best time to pray? _____

_____

How much time should you set aside to pray each day? __

_____

Farmer or Firefighter – Day 19

By Craig Duck – President/Missionary FCFInternational

Read Luke 8:11-15

Encouragement for the day – *"But the ones that fell on the good ground are those who, having heard the word with a noble and good heart, keep it and bear fruit with patience."*

Luke 8:15 NKJV

I was visiting a fire station with a friend of mine when I saw something out of the corner of my eye. Something that looked like a firefighter standing in a field with plants growing all around caught my eye. My friend laughed as he watched me, "that's their scare crow" he told me. The firefighters love to grow a garden each year, partaking of its fruits and vegetables each harvest. They use their rescue dummy dressed up as a firefighter to scare away any animal wanting to eat their food before it is ready.

In today's portion of the Bible we read a parable about another farmer. A parable is just a short story that is used to illustrate a story. Jesus often used parables to communicate His message to people. In the parable of the sower we read of a farmer who has gone out and thrown some of his seeds in his property. The seed fell on various types of soil; some by the wayside, some on rocks, some among thorns, and some on good ground. As Jesus explains this parable to His disciples we learn that the story is not about farming but rather about one's spiritual life. The Word of God is preached to many people, what they do with that word is as different as the farmer's seed. Jesus is still looking for people who will hear His words, believe on them, and then go out and bear fruit. Are you good soil?

Lord, help me to bear fruit in the fire service today. May I have the courage to share of Your great love for first responders.

Encouragement, pass it along!!

Notes

_____

_____

_____

_____

_____

_____

_____

_____

Producing Fruit – Day 20

By Wayne Detzler – International Board Member

"I am the vine; you are the branches. Those who remain in me, and I in them, will produce much fruit. For apart from me you can do nothing."

John 15:5 NLT

The secret to successful living is "remaining in Him." This is living in daily dependence on the Loving Lord. As we daily draw strength from Him, He makes our lives more and more fruitful and productive. Our lives fit in with His Word. (John 15:10) Our lives exude inexplicable joy. (John 15:11) Our lives are filled with love for others. (John 15:12-13) In other words, we are at peace with ourselves and at peace with others. Here's the secret to surviving the rough and tumble of life.

What are some ways you can better show love around the station this year? _____

_____

In what practical ways can you draw strength from God?

_____

RIT Training – Day 21

By Rob Hitt – International Board Member

"and call on me in the day of trouble; I will deliver you, and you will honor me."

Psalm 50:15 NIV

BEYOND THE BORDERS ... Last night my shift, along with neighboring departments, went through an intense R.I.T. training that simulated different obstacles that a firefighter would or could encounter, during fire ground operations. A rapid intervention team is deployed to locate and rescue a down firefighter or a firefighter that is in some type of immediate distress, better known as a "may-day". Jesus came to earth, lived a perfect life, died on a cross and rose again for our spiritual rescue. Whenever we are in distress, regardless of the circumstances or type of distress, Jesus is our ultimate "R.I.T." We can call on Him and He will respond! "Lord, increase our faith, so that when we need you or have fallen into the "entrapments" of this life, we can know that You will respond and rescue us! Amen."

How has God rescued you in the past? _____

_____

_____

Sometimes You Need a Runner – Day 22

By Craig Duck – President/Missionary FCFInternational

Read Matthew 28:11-20

Encouragement for the day – *"Therefore go and make disciples of all nations, baptizing them in the name of the Father and of the Son and of the Holy Spirit, and teaching them to obey everything I have commanded you. And surely I am with you always, to the very end of the age."*

Matthew 28:19-20 NIV

The other day we were conducting a company drill at Engine Company 11. The topic of the drill was communications at a metro incident. In Washington, DC we have a metro system that includes at grade, above ground, and tunnel portions. If there is a fire in the tunnel portion of the system firefighters have several different ways of communication. Officers can use portable radios, a dedicated conference line, or an intercom system. If all of the communication devises fail the officers in the tunnel can send a runner. The job of the runner is to repeat the order as it was given and state their authority.

In Matthew 28 we have been given the job of the runner. Our job is to find people to communicate the message to. We are told that once we find these people we are to teach them everything that Jesus has commanded us. Have you ever read the gospels? Jesus has given us a lot of information and commandments that we should be teaching others. But don't worry, He has also promised to be with us every step of the way. God has given us things in order for us to give them away. God has never intended for us to hold onto knowledge of Him. Can you imagine if there was a fire in a metro tunnel, the officer gave the runner the message, and he/she never delivered the message? Let's resolve to gladly go forth and spread the message that Jesus has given us, sharing it with other first responders.

Lord, thank you for using me to share Your message with others and for promising to be with me.

Encouragement should be standard operating procedures!!

Notes

_____

_____

_____

_____

_____

_____

Strong Refuge – Day 23

By Wayne Detzler – International Board Member

"The LORD is good, a strong refuge when trouble comes. He is close to those who trust in him."

Nahum 1:7 NLT

Thank God for this strong encouragement. Each day we face new challenges, as we navigate through life. The source of our strength is the presence of the Lord Himself. Early in the morning I was awakened to a new day, with dreaded and difficult experiences ahead. Instead of fretting, I spent some time meditating on the Lord Himself. He is our "strong refuge." Additionally, "He is our close Companion." So, we can safely trust in Him. By the time I got to the Bible, my heart was humming a hymn of praise. The Lord is good…all the time.

What are some practical ways you can reflect on the strength of God? _____

How has God come to your rescue this past year? _____

_____

The Life of a Mucker – Day 24

By Craig Duck – President/Missionary FCFInternational

Read Colossians 3:12-17

Encouragement for the day – *"And so, as those who have been chosen of God, holy and beloved, put on a heart of compassion, kindness, humility, gentleness and patience;"*

Colossians 3:12

I met a retired firefighter from Denver Colorado the other day and was able to have a conversation with him about several things. During that conversation he mentioned that our organization needs more muckers in leadership. I have never heard that expression before and asked him to explain what a mucker is. He went on to tell me that in the Denver Fire Department mucker is a term for firefighter. This retired guy from Denver went on to explain just how well respected muckers are, even though they are one of the lowest on the ladder. "The muckers are the ones that really get things done in our department; they have to because they are trying to earn the respect of the other firefighters." Without the muckers, or those who are willing to work, nothing would get done as far as he was concerned.

Christian firefighters in today's fire service need to be the muckers. Jesus Christ showed us how to demonstrate humility in the world and still be able to get things done. In today's verse we are encouraged to be compassionate to other first responders as well as show them kindness and gentleness. This can be a difficult thing to do around the station and that is why that verse goes on to say we should do all these things with patience. Men and women in the fire service need to know that there are people who are willing to help them in times of need. This is the perfect job for a Christian mucker.

Lord, help me to find someone today that I can encourage.

Encouragement, pass it on!!

Notes

_____

_____

_____

_____

_____

_____

_____

Wonderful Grace – Day 25

By Wayne Detzler – International Board Member

"But my life is worth nothing to me unless I use it for finishing the work assigned me by the Lord Jesus—the work of telling others the Good News about the wonderful grace of God."

Acts 20:24 NLT

As Paul said this, he knew that he was headed for difficult times. His freewheeling evangelistic ministry was coming to an end. Still he committed to share the Good News with those who have never heard before. This is a verse that can take us through the seasons of life from passionate youth, to productive mid-life, and beyond to the quiet years of old age.

In what ways have you been finishing the work that has been assigned to you? _____

_____

In what ways can you improve your service to the Lord in your department? _____

_____

Relational – Day 26

By Keith Helms – International Board Member

Read Matthew Chapter 22

Then one of them (the Pharisees), a lawyer, asked Him a question, testing Him, and saying, "Teacher, which is the great commandment in the law?" Jesus said to him, "'You shall love the Lord your God with all your soul, and all your mind'. This is the first and great commandment. And the second is like it: 'You shall love your neighbor as yourself.' On these two commandments hang all the Law and the Prophets." Matthew 22:35-40

Biblical truth is about relationships. God is relational within Himself; the Father, the Son, the Holy Spirit, have perfect relationship. If we believe that we are created in God's image (Gen. 1:26-27), then we must accept that we, too, are relational beings. God created each of us to love Him in worship and to love others in service. Study the scriptures so that your loving worship and loving service will continuously grow.

Notes

_____

_____

_____

Who was on the Hook? – Day 27

By Craig Duck – President/Missionary FCFInternational

Read Mark 10:35-45

Encouragement for the day – *"For even the Son of Man came not to be served but to serve, and to give his life as a ransom for many."*

Mark 10:45 ESV

Since I have been on the job in Washington, DC the one thing people want to know after a fire is "who was on the line?" The person who is "running the line" is the one who controls the nozzle and puts the fire out. When I was at Engine Company 6 we started asking people after they finished telling the story about the fire, "who was on the hook?" Everybody who has been a first responder for any length of time knows that it takes many folks to handle emergencies. Even though the lineman gets the most recognition, someone has to feed that person hose, place the pump in service, force entry, raise ladders, etc. The hookman is responsible for raising ladders, ventilating, and using their hook to pull ceilings. This position on the fire truck is just as important as the person running the line, and those tasks need to be completed in order to put a fire out.

As Christian firefighters we have to be careful desiring certain jobs. When we take on a task for our local church or for the fire service we need to examine our motives. Do we want this job to bring glory to ourselves, or are we doing it to serve the Lord. Jesus gave us the best example of servant leadership. Jesus, who is coequal with God the Father and God the Holy Spirit, came to this earth in humble circumstances. While Jesus was on the earth He served other people and not His own interests. Read the Gospels and you will discover all of Jesus's accomplishments in this life through a life of service. First responders are use to a life of serving others. Let's make sure we follow our Lord's example in serving others, especially those in our departments.

Lord, thank you for leaving us an example of how to serve others.

Encouraging those who are in need is everyone's responsibility!!

Notes

_____

_____

_____

A Hunger for God – Day 28

By Wayne Detzler – International Board Member

Heart cry for God. This sort of desperation does not go unnoticed by God. In the midst of a chaotic night in a Roman prison, the panicked Roman jailer shouts: "Sirs, what must I do to be saved?" (Acts 16:30 ESV) It is the prisoners, Paul and Silas, who respond calmly: ""Believe in the Lord Jesus, and you will be saved, you and your household." (Acts 16:31 ESV) In these days we are seeing this kind of spiritual hunger of many serious members of the Millennial generation. In a life of evangelism and revival activity, I have seldom if ever seen such a hunger for the Lord.

How have you shared your faith in Jesus to those in your department? _____

_____

How many verses about salvation can you quote from memory? _____

Who will you share your faith with this coming year? _____

_____

Three Chord Strand – Day 29

By Craig Duck – President/Missionary FCFInternational

Read Ecclesiastes 4:9-12

Encouragement for the day – *"And if one prevail against him, two shall withstand him; and a threefold cord is not quickly broken."*

Ecclesiastes 4:12 KJV

Just about every fire truck in the country has rope. Tucked away in some compartment on the apparatus is some kind of rope that is placed in a bag and ready for use. In the fire service rope has many different functions. Rope can be used for hoisting up equipment to upper floors, rescuing civilians, or pulling objects in the direction you want them to go. Over the years the rope we use has changed. Years ago first responders used manila rope with multiple strands. Today we use synthetic rope, but it still has multiple parts which makes the rope strong.

A Christian firefighter today has many people and things trying to pull them in many different directions. Some of the first responders may want you to go drinking with them. Some want you to join in with activities that you know are wrong and go against Biblical principles. Occasionally, we will even stumble and fall. The Bible encourages us to have Godly friends. In Ecclesiastes we read that a "threefold cord is not quickly broken". This threefold chord is your inner circle of Christian friends that you hang out with. Christians should seek out friends who will encourage you to read your Bible and follow God's principles and not to follow the crowd; Godly friends who will study the Bible with you and encourage you when things get tough. If you don't have Godly friends, pray that God would point them to you. Then you can become as strong as that rope you carry on your apparatus.

Lord, thank You for the friends You have given to me. Help us to be pleasing to You in everything we do.

Encourage another first responder today!!

Notes

_____

_____

_____

_____

_____

_____

_____

_____

Be Kind – Day 30

By Wayne Detzler – International Board Member

"Be kind to one another, tenderhearted, forgiving one another, as God in Christ forgave you."

Eph. 4:32 ESV

Over the years Margaret has patiently and persistently taught me this verse. Early on I discovered it was her favorite passage, her life verse. Throughout 57 years of marriage she has not only modeled this verse, but she has also taught me how to do it. In reality, the Apostle Paul here applies and demonstrates the teaching of the Lord Jesus in His Sermon on the Mount: "but if you do not forgive others their trespasses, neither will your Father forgive your trespasses." (Matt. 6:15 ESV) Jesus keeps stretching our faith . . . and our forgiveness doesn't He?

How has God stretched you over the years? _____

_____

How can you be kind in today's fire service? _____

_____

Climb for Life – Day 31

By Rob Hitt – International Board Member

"Casting all your anxieties on him, because he cares for you."

I Peter 5:7 ESV

BEYOND THE BORDERS ... Yesterday, I participated in the "Climb For Life", sponsored by the American Lung Association. Firefighters assembled teams to climb about 23 flights of stairs, in order to raise funds. During the climb, it seemed like I was never going to reach the top. (See where this is going?) However, when I finally reached the top floor, I was able to remove my gear and drink water. I was done! In the Christian life, we climb surmountable obstacles that seem like they are never going to end. But Jesus carries us through. He told us that His "burden is light". When we reach the top of our obstacles, we can then enjoy the refreshment of the LIVING water and bask in His grace and peace.

Lord, gives us strength daily to climb those heights that seem impossible at times. We know that You overcame and can release our burdens from us! Amen.

Suffering – Day 32

By Craig Duck – President/Missionary FCFInternational

Read Job 1:6-22

Encouragement for the day – *"In all this Job did not sin or charge God with wrong."*

Job 1:22 ESV

Life is full of suffering, especially in the fire service. Since I have been on the job in Washington, DC I have seen a lot of that suffering first hand. One of our dearly beloved chief's had a daughter that died in a tragic horse riding accident. That was very sad for all of us who attended that funeral. Our members have seen "good guys" get cancer and slowly die. Some of us have been on fires where our friends have died in the line of duty. Those are dark days for a department to walk through. Most of us remember 911 and how difficult it was to watch our brothers die trying to rescue so many people. Others lived that experience and still suffer from the painful memory.

When it comes to suffering, Job knows what we are going through. When you read through the real life account of Job you begin to see how much he suffered for God. Job lost his riches, his family, and his health. Job suffered tremendously as all of these trials for him came at once. All of his friends and even his wife advised him to "curse God and die". One thing that Job understood was that God cared for Job even when he went through these dark days. God cares for you and loves you just like He did for Job. In all of this terrible experience we find out that Job never blamed God and never sinned against Him. Through the suffering Job grieved for his family, prayed to his God, and waited on Him. Because of Job's love for His God, God restored Job and blessed him. God wants to do the same for us, if we let Him.

Lord, help me to fully rely on You when I go through trials and sufferings.

Encourage those who are suffering!!

Notes

_____

_____

_____

_____

_____

_____

_____

_____

_____

Committed and Faithful – Day 33

By Wayne Detzler – International Board Member

"I have no one else like Timothy, who genuinely cares about your welfare. All the others care only for themselves and not for what matters to Jesus Christ. But you know how Timothy has proved himself."

Phil. 2:20-2 NLT

Imprisoned in Rome, the Apostle Paul thanked the Lord for Timothy. Scripture shows much of Timothy's life, and he is constantly committed and faithful. As we launch a core discipleship team at Black Rock Church I am so thankful for many people like Timothy. They are spiritually solid and sincerely sharing their lives with others.

Who in your station can you demonstrate a caring attitude towards? _____

Why are first responders so self-centered in today's fire service? _____

_____

Who else in the Bible has a character like Timothy? _____

_____

The Best Gift Ever – Day 34

By Craig Duck – President/Missionary FCFInternational

Read Luke 2:1-7

Encouragement for the day – "*Then she gave birth to her firstborn Son, and she wrapped Him snugly in cloth and laid Him in a feeding trough—because there was no room for them at the lodging place.*"

Luke 2:7 Holman Christian Standard

One thing I love about the fire service is first responders giving hearts. Paid or volunteer, it doesn't matter. Go to most firehouses during the Christmas season and you will see firefighters collecting Christmas presents for children in need. Whether it is for their community or part of the Marines toys for tots program, firefighters always seem to give the most and best gifts. I can just imagine some young child opening up one of those gifts at Christmas. The joy that it must bring to that child would be great to see.

The Bible tells us of the best gift that was ever given to man. God sent us a gift some 2,000 years ago because of His great love for us. God sent Jesus, His only Son, as a baby wrapped in swaddling clothes and laid in a manger. This same Jesus would grow up and lead a perfect life without sin. Not everyone was happy with this gift from God and certain men rejected the Savior and crucified Him. Jesus was buried and three days later rose from the dead and is currently seated at the right hand of the Father. Because of Jesus's perfect sacrifice we can have forgiveness of our sins and be allowed into heaven. Now that is the best gift ever.

Lord thank you for the best gift ever that was given to me by Jesus Christ. Help me to share this gift with other first responders.

Encouragement, setting the standard in the fire service!!

Notes

_____

_____

_____

_____

_____

_____

_____

_____

God of Peace – Day 35

By Wayne Detzler – International Board Member

"The God of peace will soon crush Satan under your feet. May the grace of our Lord Jesus be with you."

Rom. 16:20 NLT

Years ago, I was preaching in a small church in Luxembourg, and I needed an encouragement for them. The Lord gave me this verse. No matter how fragile we feel or look, the victory is ours through our Lord Jesus Christ. This is His encouragement even in the midst of strong spiritual warfare and against demonic powers: "This is the spirit of the antichrist, which you heard was coming and now is in the world already. Little children, you are from God and have overcome them, for he who is in you is greater than he who is in the world." (1 John 4:3-4 ESV)

What struggles have you gone through in the past year? _

_____

_____

How can we keep our focus on Christ during difficult times in our station? _____

_____

Pigpen – Day 36

By Keith Helms – International Board Member

Read I Corinthians Chapter 2

I worked many years with a firefighter who was affectionately called "pigpen". He has never been asked to be one of the Charlotte Fire Department models at a charity fashion show. He has never been assigned to temporarily fill in for the department's PIO. However, when I pulled up on a rocking structure fire and I knew that he was on the nozzle, then I had full confidence that we were ok. When he was attacking the fire, I wasn't concerned about any wrinkles in his uniform, whether he had polished his boots that morning, or if he had combed his hair that week. No, I was thankful that one of the best firefighters this department has ever seen was knocking down the fire.

Sometimes it is easy for us to lose sight of the big picture. We get too caught up in dress code policies and other secondary issues, losing sight of our main mission. Pigpen may not win the "Best Dressed" award, but I've never seen anyone better at interior firefighting. His mission is to save lives and property; it is not to look like Brad Pitt.

In ministries, we can make the mistake of strategizing too much about secondary things and drift away from our primary mission. We try to develop entertaining ways to draw people in. We spend too much time and energy looking for new, exciting programs that will increase our numbers. While I am not saying that the secondary things are of no importance, let's be certain that we are first seeking to glorify God in the fire service through evangelism and discipleship. Read 1 Cor. 2:1-2. Read the FCFInternational Vision and Mission Statements. Our ministry is not about promoting ourselves (or our ministry) and looking good. FCFInternational is about God Almighty and glorifying Him. That is our daily call.

How can you stay focused for Christ in a fire service that has so many demands? _____

_____

Which Godly character of the Bible would you like most to emulate? _____

_____

Notes

_____

_____

_____

Remembering Zadock – Day 37

By Craig Duck – President/Missionary FCFInternational

Read Ezekiel 48:10-15

Encouragement for the day – *"This shall be for the consecrated priests, the sons of Zadok, who kept my charge, who did not go astray when the people of Israel went astray, as the Levites did"*

Ezekiel 48:11 ESV

What is in a name? This morning as I was reading my devotions I came across a name we don't hear too often in today's fire service, Zadok. When I read that name I immediately recalled our fire departments yearly memorial service where we honor firefighters who have died in the line of duty. During the ceremony we read the names of the fallen. One of those names is of a private named Zadok. I often wondered where that name came from and what the meaning of the name is. In the fire service names are important. Certain names are associated with heroic deeds, or distinguished careers. We often recant stories to younger firefighters of big fires or lives saved by certain firefighters. We are quick to tell of the names of individuals who sometimes are labeled as cowards or not good first responders.

58

Today's verse tells us the importance of the name Zadok. If you have read through the book of Ezekiel you will remember how angry God was at His people Israel. They had defiled the name of God and committed wicked sins in the land. God decided to throw His people out of the land and into the hands of their enemy. After a period of time Ezekiel was shown how the remnant of Israel was to be restored. This is where we hear how the sons of Zadok did not go astray during this wicked period in Israel. What an awesome testimony by Zadock and his sons, standing firm for God during evil times. I am confident that if good old Zadok were a first responder today he would still have an untarnished testimony for God. So how are you doing? What do people think when they hear your name. If you need help changing your life around go to God for help, He is the one Zadok and his sons looked to for their day to day strength.

Lord, thank You for examples in the Bible that encourage us to press on no matter what are circumstances are.

Encouragement is contagious, pass it on!

Not Ashamed – Day 38

By Wayne Detzler – International Board Member

> *"The message of the cross is foolish to those who are headed for destruction! But we who are being saved know it is the very power of God."*
>
> 1 Cor. 1:18 NLT

The Good News of Jesus Christ is not understood apart from the work of the Holy Spirit. However, when the Holy Spirit opens our hearts and minds, it becomes the best news we ever heard. For those who believe, the gospel is the power of God unto salvation. This was always a theme of Paul's ministry. "For I am not ashamed of this Good News about Christ. It is the power of God at work, saving everyone who believes—the Jew first and also the Gentile." (Rom. 1:16 NLT)

What did Jesus call those who did not believe His message of salvation? _____

_____

Why did Jesus have to die to pay the penalty for our sins?

_____

_____

In the Valleys – Day 39

By Robb Hitt – International Board Member

"Be still, and know that I am God;
I will be exalted among the nations,
I will be exalted in the earth!"

Psalm 46:10 NKJV

In the movie "Sound of Music", Maria the nun makes the statement, "When God closes a door, He opens a window." Even though this statement isn't found in scripture, it still holds practical applications for the believer. I am in the process of transitioning from EMT-I to Advanced-EMT. This process has proven difficult and very tedious. However, it is in these valleys that the Lord whispers, "Be still and know that I am God." The key to that verse is "BE STILL". Easier said than done, huh? But His grace is indeed sufficient. Please pray for me, as I prepare to take my AEMT written exam. Praise the Lord for His unending mercies!

How has God stretched you in your walk with Christ? _____
_____

In what ways can you better listen to the still small voice of God in your life? _____

Pressing On – Day 40

By Craig Duck – President/Missionary FCFInternational

Read Philippians 3:1-16

Encouragement for the day – *"That I may know him, and the power of his resurrection, and the fellowship of his sufferings, being made conformable unto his death;"*

Philippians 3:10 KJV

I have been involved in the fire service for over 30 years. During that time I have seen many changes and have gone through some rough times. Some of the worst times are when our department has experienced a line of duty death. During those times it is like life has stopped. You don't notice anything that is going on around you. You are unaware of what is happening in the community, politics, or even your own family. You become so focused on making sure the family of the deceased has their needs met, the company is prepared for the funeral, and that you as a leader are able to instill hope for those you serve with.

As Christian firefighters we have a resource available to us that will allow us to bring hope during those difficult times. That hope is eternal life through Jesus Christ our Lord. Paul, the author of Philippians, shares his heart and purpose with his readers. This joyful attitude never diminished over time, even during difficult days. What is this joyful attitude you might ask? "That I might know him, and the power of his resurrection, and the fellowship of his sufferings, being made conformable unto his death." Because of his relationship with his Savior, Paul was able to press on during difficult days in order that he might have the joy of knowing his Savior that much better. When we allow God to work in us He will give us the strength to carry on. Let's joyfully rely on the strength of God in order to press on when we feel like giving up.

Lord, help me to know you better.

Encouragement should be our standard operating guideline!!

Notes

_____

_____

_____

_____

_____

_____

_____

_____

Proclaiming Righteousness – Day 41

By Wayne Detzler – International Board Member

An anonymous psalmist writes: *"My life is an example to many, because you have been my strength and protection. That is why I can never stop praising you; I declare your glory all day long."*

Psalm 71:7-8 NLT

People who come to know Christ cannot stop talking about it. They are so amazed at the good grace of God. This week we celebrate the life of our dear friend, Sue Koczak. Throughout her 100 years of life she lit up the world around her with a bright witness to God's grace. Most of her adult life was spent as the widowed mother of twin daughters, and Joyce and Janet stand as living witness to Sue's stunning faith. The psalmist finishes with this ringing affirmation: "I will tell everyone about your righteousness. All day long I will proclaim your saving power." (Psalm 71:15 NLT)

In what ways are you working on your lasting testimony?

_____

_____

_____

Standing Against Adversities – Day 42

By Rob Hitt – International Board Member

Read I Samuel Chapter 17

As believers, we need to stand against the adversities and issues that plague the church today. When the world and all the satanic forces display a challenge to us on a daily basis, we can go answer these challenges in the power of the Lord. Goliath challenged the Israelites day by day, showing his physical size and barking out threats to intimidate them. It worked! However, a shepherd had faith, looking past his fears and the intimidating factors that surrounded him, looking to the Lord for strength.

Let us answer the world and the challenges that we face daily as David did; "... Is there not a cause?" I Samuel 17:29. Through his faith in the Lord, he overcame insurmountable obstacles. Even through David's failures, Jesus called him, a man after God's own heart." We face many "Goliath's" in our walk with the Lord. Even though we may not use a sling and a stone, we DO have the same victory as David did. We can also have the same FAITH that David did. May we strive to face OUR giants through the power of the Holy Spirit and not our own. Lord bless us, as we continue forward, doing His will until He comes.

K.I.S.S. – Day 43

By Craig Duck – President/Missionary FCFInternational

Read II Corinthians 1:8-14

Encouragement for the day – *"For we are not writing to you anything other than what you read and understand and I hope you will fully understand"*

II Corinthians 1:13 ESV

When I first joined the fire service back in the early eighties I learned a valuable lesson that has stuck with me. That principle is the K.I.S.S. principle, keep it simple silly. The fire service is not complicated. Put the wet stuff on the red stuff, if it is bleeding stop it, if they're not breathing get them started. Maybe I am just getting old, but it seems like folks in leadership today are violating the K.I.S.S. principle and making things way over complicated. Even James Madison, our fourth President, understood this principle when he helped draft the constitution. President Madison warned against creating laws "so voluminous that they cannot be read or so incoherent that they cannot be understood".

When we share the gospel with other first responders it is important to remember the K.I.S.S. principle. Don't try and overcomplicate the message that

God has given us. Remember that God's message of eternal life is as easy as ABC. Acknowledge that you are a sinner, "for all have sinned and come short of the glory of God" (Romans 3:23). You can also share what the penalty of our sins are, Romans 6:23. Believe, "believe on the Lord Jesus Christ and you will be saved, you and your household" (Acts 16:31). Confess, "If we confess our sins, He is faithful and just to forgive us our sins and to cleanse us from all unrighteousness" (I John 1:9). So simple a child can read and believe.

Lord, thank you for your message of eternal life. Help me to share it with other first responders.

Encouraging first responders to keep the faith!!

Notes

_____

_____

_____

_____

_____

_____

_____

_____

Songs of Joy – Day 44

By Wayne Detzler – International Board Member

"Songs of joy and victory are sung in the camp of the godly. The strong right arm of the Lord has done glorious things."

Psalm 118:15 NLT

Joyful worship always rings out from God's people. It is our response to the presence and power of the Lord in our lives. Across the country we are hearing reports of God's blessing among Millennial young people. As a result they are producing exciting new worship songs. Today is the Lord's Day, and we have a chance to join the song. As the psalmist writes: "The Lord is my strength and my song; he has given me victory." (Psalm 118:14 NLT)

Does your life song sing forth the praises of the Lord? ___

_____

If not, in what ways can you improve you circumstances in order to begin to proclaim the mighty works of God? _____

_____

What "glorious things" has God accomplished in your life?

_____

Spiritual 360 – Day 45

By Keith Helms – International Board Member

"Search me, O God, and know my heart; Try me, and know my anxieties; and see if there is any wicked way in me, and lead me in the way everlasting."

Psalm 139: 23-24 NKJV

When the first officer arrives on the scene of a structure fire, he (or she) should be concerned about what is observed. Officers should also be concerned about what is not seen. As soon as possible, officers need to get a 360 so they can give a report about all sides of the structure. The rear of the structure will often present additional problems or additional capabilities. If we only look at what we presently see, then we limit ourselves in effectively controlling the incident.

Our daily walk with Christ is similar. We should always aggressively fight against the sin in our lives that we observe. However, we should also acknowledge that the unobserved sin can pose a greater problem. We need a spiritual 360. Psalm 139:23-24 gives us the resource. Be constant in asking the Holy Spirit to reveal to you what is hidden and unobserved.

Guidance System – Day 46

By Craig Duck – President/Missionary FCFInternational

Read Psalm 27

Encouragement for the day – *"Wait on the Lord; be of good courage, and He shall strengthen your heart; wait, I say, on the Lord!"*

Psalm 27:14 NKJV

In the District of Columbia Fire and EMS Department our drivers know their box alarm areas. In order to be a technician for a company a firefighter has to study their district and take a test. Almost every tour our folks are studying their area in order to know where they are going. This saves a lot of time on emergency calls as the driver does not have to look up on a map where the company is going. The company I work with is one of the paramedic engine companies. Occasionally, we will be sent way out of our district. Fortunately, we have a guidance system, a GPS, which will help us to get there. All I have to do is touch the screen where it reads "Map" and it will guide us to the emergency.

Life is full of choices. In the fire service first responders are trying to get you to go a different direction than what God would have you to go. When we need

God's guidance He is always there for us. Christian first responders can activate this guidance system by meditating on God's Word the Bible. God promises that His Word will be a light to our path (Psalm 119:105). We need to regularly read the Bible and be willing to humble ourselves and submit to its teaching (I Peter 5:6). Our guidance system also has the capability to listen to us and answer our questions. We are told in I John 5:14 and 15 that if we need guidance we can pray to God and He will answer our prayers according to His will. So don't take someone else's advice on how to live your life, look to God's guidance system, the Bible, for all of your answers.

Lord, help me to faithfully read and obey your Word.

Encouraging one another to keep the faith!!

Notes

_____

_____

_____

_____

Unfailing Love – Day 47

By Wayne Detzler – International Board Member

"Your unfailing love, O LORD, is as vast as the heavens; your faithfulness reaches beyond the clouds."

Psalm 36:5 NLT

The awesome scope of God's love is described here in universal terms. With today's super telescopes we can probe the limits of our universe, but nothing can reach the limits of God's love. When Jesus explained His coming and His sacrifice on our behalf, He said the source was God's great love. (John 3:16; John 4:10) Even when God's people suffered indescribable humiliation at the hands of the Babylonian barbarians, God's love comforted and encouraged them. "The faithful love of the LORD never ends! His mercies never cease. Great is his faithfulness; his mercies begin afresh each morning." (Lam 3:22-23 NLT) Simply stated, we cannot escape the love of God. Still remembering the old hymn from last Sunday at Black Rock Church: "How marvelous, how wonderful, is my Savior's love for me."

How has God encouraged you with His great love? _____

_____

Dying to Self – Day 48

Keith Helms – International Board Member

"Greater love has no one than this, that someone lay down his life for his friends."

John 15:13 ESV

These words are often used by firefighters to express their willingness to sacrifice their lives at a fire; and this is a noble thought. Anytime that a firefighter dies at the scene of a fire, we should see that as a self-sacrificial act of love. However, I think that the verse may actually be speaking about a different concept of "laying down your life" that is actually more difficult.

In John 15, Christ was describing to His disciples the picture of Him being the vine and His followers being the branches. The branch relies on the vine for everything and can do nothing without the vine. Christ then spoke of the love between Him and the Father and He encouraged them to join in with this love. That is led to the words of verse 13. Consider the possibility that Christ may be referring to the call to die daily to self. The same thought is presented in Luke 9:23-24; "Then He said to them all, 'If anyone desires to come after Me, let him deny himself, and take up his cross daily, and follow Me. For those who want to save their life will lose it, and those who lose their life for my sake will save it.'" While I am not suggesting that dying at a fire is not an act of love, I am suggesting that a greater act of love is to die to self, daily. This means that you willingly set aside your own desires and needs for the good of others. This is what Christ demonstrated in His birth, death, and resurrection. Paul wrote about this in Philippians 2:1-11. If you want to be a disciple of Christ, you must die to self; you must set aside your own desires and seek to serve Christ. This is how fruit is produced. We (the branches) trust completely in Christ (the vine) to provide all that we need which enables us to focus on others (the fruit).

Is dying at a fire an act of love? Absolutely. Is that the greatest act of love? Consider that the greater act of love may be to die daily; to live as Christ lived; to love humbly as He loved. To me, this is a much more costly death. Instead of being honored in this world, it is actually discouraged. The world suggests that you take care of yourself first. Christ suggests the opposite. We are called to die to this world; live for the next world; and to live a life that reflects the image of Christ while we are here. While you may not receive the praise of others in the daily dying to self, you will receive the pleasure of the Lord God Almighty. Whose praise are you seeking?

Get the Ice Pack – Day 49

By Craig Duck – President/Missionary FCFInternational

Read Hebrews 10:11-25

Encouragement for the day – *"And let us consider one another in order to stir up love and good works, not forsaking the assembling of ourselves together, as is the manner of some, but exhorting one another, and so much more as you see the Day approaching."*

Hebrews 10:24-25 NKJV

"Get an icepack" is heard commonly on medical locals. Icepacks are typically used to keep the swelling down on injuries in order to prevent further injury and provide some comfort to the patient. Icepacks are also used to cool down patients who are suffering from heat related emergencies. The icepack is a simple tool that sits in most first aid bags carried on emergency vehicles. The icepack sits at room temperature until someone breaks open the enclosed plastic tube that contains the water which then mixes with the ammonia nitrate. Once the two chemicals mix together an endothermic reaction takes place and the liquid becomes cold. As long as the two chemicals remain apart the cold pack will remain room temperature.

The Fellowship of Christian Firefighters Internationals key verse is Hebrews 10:25-25. We understand that if Christians don't regularly meet together for fellowship, encouragement, and Bible study, their lives will remain stagnant. When Christians meet together they will ultimately stir one another up for love and good works, similar to the action of a cold pack. Our desire is for every member to be actively involved in a local church of their choosing. Knowing that first responders can better relate to each other, our other desire is to meet together in local chapters. The Bible places an emphasis on meeting together and then going out and meeting other people's needs (love and good works). As time is getting closer and closer to "the Day" (the end of the world) we need to be diligent about encouraging one another. How about you, are you regularly meeting with other Christians in your local church and at your station?

Lord, help me to regularly meet with other first responders in order that we might encourage one another to serve You better.

Encouraging first responders to keep the faith!!

A Simple Prayer – Day 50

By Wayne Detzler – International Board Member

"I entrust my spirit into your hand."

Psalm 31:5 NLT

This simple phrase resonates throughout the Scripture in very dramatic settings. When Jesus was dying on the cross, these were His last words. (Luke 23:46) As the stones rained down on the head of Stephen, he too cried out these words. (Acts 7:59) Actually, most Jewish children knew them as a bedtime prayer. As a final act of worship after a long day of play the little ones would utter this short prayer: "I entrust my spirit into your hand." This common call to God gained uncommon meaning on the parched, dying lips of the Lord. Jesus. Prayer is the practice of faith and the promise of hope.

Have you ever come to a place in your Christian walk where you have entrusted your spirit into God's hand? ___

_____

How has God blessed you since that time? _____

_____

Crystal Clear – Day 51

Rob Hitt – International Board Member

Read Psalm 119:17-24

BEYOND THE BORDERS ... A basic truth: God's hand is not shortened that He cannot redeem! I went to the eye doctor today, for a routine check-up. As always, I had drops put in, so my pupils would dilate for the examination. Shortly after, everything was blurry. I was then given prescription reading glasses. When I put them on, everything was crystal clear! That is how it is with the heart of man. In a sinful life style away from the Lord, life is disorganized and "blurry". However, when our spiritual eyes are opened at salvation, we see things very clear. We begin to see things as God sees them. As the scales were removed from Paul's eyes physically, the Lord can remove the scales of sin from one's heart spiritually!

"Lord, please open our eyes to the mission field of the world; that those within it, may come to a saving knowledge of you. Amen."

Notes

_____

_____

Dump Valve – Day 52

By Craig Duck – President/Missionary FCFInternational

Read Romans 5:1-11

Encouragement for the day – "And hope does not put us to shame, because God's love has been poured into our hearts through the Holy Spirit who has been given to us."

Romans 5:5 ESV

I have been a firefighter in the District of Columbia Fire and EMS Department for the past 28 years. Since we work in an urban environment, our department's standard operating guidelines reflect the type of emergencies we respond to. One type of operation we are not proficient at is tanker operations. Our department does not have any tankers and most of our members have never even seen a dump valve. Dump valves are placed on tankers for the purpose of rapidly pouring the water into a portable pond. Without this valve, valuable time would be wasted waiting for the water to fill up the portable pond.

The Christian first responder has had the love of God "poured into our hearts through the Holy Spirit" if we have put our faith and trust in Jesus Christ for the forgiveness of sins. Our new life in Christ brings us peace with God and affords us the opportunity for the Holy Spirit to live within us. As we live out our faith in the fire service we will have the power of God living within us to help guide us during challenging situations. Paul reminds us that our trials have been placed before us in order that they may produce character and perseverance in our lives. The more grace that the first responder needs the more is available through God's "dump valve". Why does God do this? God provides grace to first responders because of His great love for us.

Lord, thank You for Your great love for me. Help me today to live out my faith in the department You have called me to.

Encouraging the fire service to keep the faith!!

Notes

_____

_____

_____

_____

_____

_____

_____

_____

Bringing People to Jesus – Day 53

By Wayne Detzler – International Board Member

"Then they came to Philip, who was from Bethsaida of Galilee, and asked him, saying, 'Sir, we wish to see Jesus.'"

John 12:21 NKJV

It was the last Passover, and Jesus was only days away from the cross. Some Greeks came to see Jesus. True to his character, Philip simply led them to Jesus. It's a touching personal story. Many years ago I was preaching at Judson Baptist Church in Oak Park, IL. As I stepped to the pulpit two things struck me. First, the beautiful pulpit was a gift in memory of Margaret's uncle, Robert Eddy. Second, there was a plaque only the preacher could see. It said: "Sir, we would see Jesus." (John 12:21 KJV) Like Philip, let's make sure we always bring people to Jesus.

Have you brought someone to Jesus lately? _____

_____

If you haven't, in what ways can you recommit to this command to share the Gospel with first responders in the fire service? _____

_____

What Things Make You Angry? – Day 54

Keith Helms – International Board Member

For most of us, we would say that other people or other things make us angry. Actually, you make yourself angry. You see someone or something that is not right in your eyes, and you quickly react with an internal firestorm. We typically don't think of it as a choice to be angry, but we are not angry until after we have processed the event through our mind. It is most often a split-second processing, but it does involve a choice. The Bible alludes to righteous and unrighteous anger. Righteous anger is anything that angers us that also angers God. The scriptures refer to God being angry at evil, anything that disregards His glory, and our failure to trust Him completely. Unrighteous anger generally results when we feel that our glory has been offended, when things or people don't cooperate with our personal agenda. Unrighteous anger is rooted in pride and self-protection. A key to controlling your anger is to be aware of the agendas that tend to float through your idle mind. Are you more focused on God and His glory or you and your own glory? Do you have an ongoing compassion for others? Do you fight the battle of easily seeing the sins in others while denying the sin in your flesh? Seek to view others through the lens of compassion and forgiveness.

Set your mind on Christ and seek to limit your anger to the things that make Him angry. It is your choice.

For additional study, meditate on these passages: Ezekiel 36:20-38; Ex. 4:4; Num. 25:3; Judges 2:14; 2 Kings 3:3; Matt. 21:12-13; Rom. 8; Rom. 12:17-21; Eph. 4:26-32; Col. 3:1-17; James 4:1-6

What things typically make you angry? _____

_____

_____

_____

What are some practical ways to deal with inappropriate anger? _____

_____

_____

_____

Notes

_____

_____

_____

_____

_____

_____

A Do Over – Day 55

By Craig Duck – President/Missionary FCFInternational

Read John 21:1-19

Encouragement for the day – *"So when they had eaten breakfast, Jesus said to Simon Peter, "Simon, son of Jonah, do you love Me more than these?" He said to Him, "Yes, Lord; You know that I love You." He said to him, "Feed My Lambs."*

John 21:15 NKJV

We all make mistakes, especially those of us in the fire service. During our time together in a busy engine company, Charlie and I went to a lot of fires. Most of the time, we were able to put out the fires we went to. On one particular fire, which happened to be four houses down from the firehouse, we messed up. When we pulled in front of the house we had fire showing on the first and second floors. Charlie and I stretched the line and began to extinguish the fire. We were able to knock down the fire on the first floor and were getting to move up to the second floor. The problem was, we couldn't find the stairs. Try as we may, we could not locate those stairs. The chief finally pulled us out and we went to exterior operations. After the fire we felt embarrassed as the stairs were right behind the front door. We wished we had a do over button on that one.

In today's text, we learn of how Peter was given a do over from Jesus. As Peter watched Jesus being dragged to prison, he denied the Lord three times in front of other people in order to watch what was going on. Feeling miserable about what he did, Peter went back to fishing. Now that the Lord had been resurrected, He appeared to His disciples in order to encourage them. During breakfast Jesus asked Peter three times, "Do you love me?" Peter got the message and Jesus was able to restore Peter to a right relationship with Him. Jesus continues to give do overs to those of us in the fire service. When we mess things up, we can go to Jesus and ask for forgiveness. We, like Peter, can then restore our relationship with the Lord.

Lord, thank You that we can be forgiven and have a right relationship with You.

Encouragement is our standard operating guideline (SOG)!!

Notes

_____

_____

God Cares – Day 56

By Wayne Detzler – International Board Member

"Whoever mocks the poor shows contempt for their Maker; whoever gloats over disaster will not go unpunished."

Prov. 17:5 NIV

It's amazing that King Solomon would pen these words, but he brings a powerful message. God cares about the poor, and God loves each individual. The basis of this teaching is in creation itself. Each person is here because God is the Creator, and this gives dignity to each individual. Then he adds these words: "Whoever is kind to the poor lends to the LORD, and he will reward them for what they have done. (Prov. 19:17 NIV) My mind flashes back to Beijing, and the little children who sit on the streets begging. I pray that someone will crouch down beside them and help them. If I could go back I would attempt to learn their language and bring them the love of Jesus.

In what ways have you shown the love of God to the poor?

_____

How can Christian first responders do a better job in sharing our riches to poor departments? _____

The Cross – Day 57

Keith Helms – International Director

"Then he called the crowd to him along with his disciples and said: "Whoever wants to be my disciple must deny themselves and take up their cross and follow me."

Mark 8:34 NIV

Consider these words from John Charles Ryle on the cross of Christ: "You must know His cross . . . or else you will die in your sins.

Unless you know the power of Christ's cross by experience . . . unless you are willing to confess that your salvation depends entirely on the work that Christ did upon the cross . . . Christ will profit you nothing.

Beware . . . of a religion without the cross. There are hundreds of places of worship . . . in which there is everything almost except the cross; . . . there are thousands of religious books . . . in which there is everything except the cross.

If Christ had not gone to the cross and suffered in our stead, the Just for the unjust, there would not have been a spark of hope for us."

Accountability – Day 58

By Craig Duck – President/Missionary FCFInternational

Read Psalm 119:9-16

Encouragement for the day –*"How can a young man keep his way pure? By guarding it according to your word."*

Psalm 119:9 ESV

Over the past several years the fire service has taken the lead on the Incident Command System (ICS). Part of ICS is the accountability of everyone working in the hot zone. The incident commander is required to know where every company is working within five minutes of the incident. This is accomplished as he/she sectors out the incident and communicates with the companies. At the 10 minute mark the incident commander is responsible for conducting a formal roll call. This is accomplished by directly talking with the group and division leaders who will state the companies working with them, the number of people, and their current location. An accountability system has been developed because of firefighters who have died in the line of duty. When incident commanders choose not to utilize the accountability system they risk the loss of more lives.

God has also set up a system of accountability. This accountability system is called the Bible. The Bible is a book that was written by holy men of God under the inspiration of the Holy Spirit. That is why some folks refer to the Bible as God breathed. II Timothy 3:16 states; "All Scripture is breathed out by God and profitable for teaching, for reproof, for correction, and for training in righteousness, (ESV). When the Bible is regularly read by believers it keeps us from going contrary to Gods will for our lives. The Bible is our accountability system. When we choose not to read it, we put ourselves in a dangerous position. Have you been reading your Bible lately?

Lord, help me to regularly read Your word the Bible.

Encouragement is everybody's assignment!!

Notes

_____

_____

_____

_____

_____

_____

_____

Learner – Day 59

By Wayne Detzler – International Board Member

"Now there was a disciple at Damascus named Ananias. The Lord said to him in a vision, 'Ananias.' And he said, 'Here I am, Lord.'"

Acts 9:10 ESV

It is intriguing that Luke refers to Ananias as a "disciple." Throughout this powerful story of Saul/Paul's conversion, the believers in Damascus are called "disciples." (Acts 9:19, 25 ESV) In Greek the word, "disciple" is Mathetes. It means a "learner." It's my prayer that every day I will grow as a disciple and learner of the Lord Jesus.

What was the last portion of the Bible that you thoroughly read and studied? _____

Matthew 28:18-20 is one of the famous portions of the Bible that encourages disciples to go and make other disciples. In what ways have you been obedient to that command? _____
_____

Do you have a learner's heart? _____

Great Joys – Day 60

By Keith Helms – International Board Member

Consider this: When I was a company officer, one of the joys was to see one of the firefighters on our truck get promoted to captain. This was especially true when I was able to witness the change that began when a rookie firefighter was assigned to our truck. I felt that it was my responsibility to ensure that they were well prepared for their current position and future new positions. I wanted to instill in them a level of expertise and confidence that enabled them to be effective as a new officer. Of course, "You can't make a silk purse out of a sow's ear" (Mrs. Wiley referring to Ernest T. Bass).

This analogy paints a good portrait of our discipleship ministry. Effective discipleship is based on the God's transforming work of changing us from the "old man" to the "new man" when we believe in Jesus Christ as our savior. We are no longer a "sow's ear". A young believer and a rookie firefighter are similar. Both have tremendous potential; both can become a "silk purse". It is the responsibility of the company officer to teach, train, and encourage the young firefighter to mature beyond the status of being a rookie. The firefighter's responsibility is to desire maturity and obey the teaching of his officer. Similarly, a young believer must have the desire to mature and he must obey God's call to sanctification. It is the call of spiritually mature believers to teach, train, and encourage him so that he no longer remains a "rookie" in God's Kingdom. The goal of our Discipleship Ministry is spiritual maturity of believers, resulting in disciples who make disciples, who make disciples, and so on, all to the glory of God.

To get a biblical perspective of discipleship, study John 14:1-16:33. A key verse is 15:8. "By this My Father is glorified, that you bear much fruit; so you will be My disciples."

You can join with us in the ministry of making disciples of Christ. The curriculum is found on our website (fellowshipofchristianfirefighters.org) in the Training section. Your joy in witnessing the growth of a young believer will be eternal.

Who can you pray about beginning a "one on one" discipleship ministry in your department? _____

_____

What is holding you back from discipling another firefighter? _____

_____

_____

_____

Demonstration Time – Day 61

By Craig Duck – President/Missionary FCFInternational

Read I Corinthians 2:1-16

Encouragement for the day – *"And my speech and my preaching were not with persuasive words of human wisdom, but in demonstration of the Spirit and of power."*

I Corinthians 2:4 NKJV

I love going to the fire shows that are hosted in various parts of the country. When you go to these shows you will find new products that are being sold by the manufacturers. The manufacturers typically have someone at the show who will demonstrate to anyone that will listen about the new product. Over the year's manufactures and fire service leaders have discovered that first responders typically will not learn from words only. If you want a firefighter to understand about a concept or new tool you have to demonstrate it for them. Once they see what you are describing in action they are more likely to buy into the idea.

Paul took a similar approach to his ministry when sharing about salvation through Jesus Christ. Paul knew that if he only preached the gospel to the Corinthians with words, not many of them would be saved. Paul decided to demonstrated the power of God through his actions; he backed up everything he said by how he lived his life before the Corinthians. As Christian firefighters we should ask God each day to help us "walk worthy" before other firefighters. When we allow God to work through us it is a more powerful demonstration than any words we could muster up.

Lord, use me today in my fire station. Help me to demonstrate your love for first responders.

Together, let's make encouragement in the fire service a standard operating guideline!!

Notes

_____

_____

_____

_____

_____

_____

_____

_____

Perfect in Weakness – Day 62

By Wayne Detzler – International Board Member

"And He said to me, 'My grace is sufficient for you, for My strength is made perfect in weakness.' Therefore most gladly I will rather boast in my infirmities, that the power of Christ may rest upon me."

2 Cor. 12:9 NKJV

This is one of those amazing apparent contradictions. How can it be? The secret is simple. It is the presence and power of God. At my weakest, God is at His strongest. And all this happens in the small sphere of my little human life. Paul concludes: "For when I am weak, then I am strong." (2 Cor. 12:10 NKJV) It allows me to pray a big prayer. The Holy Spirit has been teaching me to pray this prayer in every situation: "Loving Father, do the thing in this situation or this person's life that brings the most glory to You." This has led to absolute freedom in prayer.

Have you ever come to a point in your life where you surrendered all to God? _____

Explain how that has changed your life. _____

_____

_____

Eternal Life – Day 63

By Keith Helms – International Board Member

Is it possible to know for certain that you are going to heaven? According to the Bible, the answer is yes (1 John 5:13). You can be certain of your salvation. Here is God's plan for your salvation:

You may be familiar with the well-known verse, John 3:16. It states, "For God so loved the world that He gave His only begotten Son, that whoever believes in Him should not perish but have everlasting life." So what does this mean for us?

God (the Father, the Son, and the Holy Spirit) loves all of mankind. His love is offered as a free gift. We can do nothing to earn it. However, God does hate sin and He will allow nothing evil to enter into Heaven (Revelation 21:27; Psalm 5:4). Therefore, man must be perfect to enter Heaven. Herein lies our problem. No one can honestly say that they are perfect. Although you may feel that you are better than your coworker, you have to admit that you have fallen short of the mark of perfection. Everyone has sinned (Romans, 3:10, 3:23; Isaiah 53:6; Ecclesiastes 7:20). You cannot be "good enough" to enter Heaven. So what must we do and how can we enter Heaven if we must be perfect? The only thing that we can do is to receive Christ's perfection as a free gift (Ephesians 2:8-9; Titus 3:5; Romans 6:23; John 10:28). There is only one condition for receiving eternal life. You must believe in Jesus Christ as your personal Savior. You must believe that when He died on the cross, He completely paid for all of your sins (John 3:18, 5:24, 6:47, 20:31; 2 Corinthians 5:21; 1 Peter 3:18; Acts 16:31; 1 Corinthians 15:1-4). Furthermore, there is no "Plan B" or any other additional plans. Eternal Salvation is based only in belief in Christ (John 14:6; Acts 4:10-12).

God wants you to have eternal life with Him. His desire is that everyone be saved (1 Timothy 2:3-4). However, you must believe in God's plan of salvation to receive eternal life with Him. If you do believe in Christ, according to the Bible you will be given eternal life with God and become a part of God's family (John 1:12). This is our hope for you. If you have any questions about this or if you want to discuss where you will spend eternity, please contact us.

Notes

_____

_____

_____

_____

_____

Just Kids – Day 64

By Craig Duck – President/Missionary FCFInternational

Read I Timothy chapter 4

Encouragement for the day – *"Let no man despise thy youth; but be thou an example of the believers, in word, in conversation, in charity, in spirit, in faith, in purity."*

I Timothy 4:12 KJV

     I walked into a friend's firehouse one day and saw a bunch of kids cleaning and painting the kitchen area. When my friend came walking in I asked when their department started a junior firefighters program. After my friend finished laughing he told me that these kids were assigned here. Situations like that really make you feel older. It seems like just yesterday when I started in the fire service, now folks are looking to me as the older Lieutenant.

     In the Bible we find a lot of people who courageously followed after God when they were young. David was seventeen when he was anointed as King and not much older when he went up against Goliath. Joseph was also a teenager when he was pressed into service for God. Mary, the mother of Jesus, was also only a teenager when she was told by an Angel that she would give birth to the Savior. Often in the fire service some of us older firefighters look down on the younger firefighters. The Bible encourages us to act differently towards "the Kids" in the station. The older firefighters need to teach the younger firefighters on how to do the job. The younger firefighters should not get discouraged, but rather should be an example to firefighters who do not believe in Jesus Christ as Lord and Savior. Everything the young Christian firefighter does should point others to God.

Lord, help me to be a Godly example to other firefighters today. Help me to be the best firefighter I can for You.

Encouragement, pass it on!!

Notes

_____

_____

_____

_____

_____

_____

_____

_____

Real Worship – Day 65

By Wayne Detzler – International Board Member

"Holy, holy, holy is the Lord God, the Almighty—
the one who always was, who is, and who is still to come."

Rev. 4:8 NLT

We all want to worship the Lord better, and the Scripture gives us clues. This is one of the songs sung in heaven, and it focuses on the holiness of God. Notice the absence of any reference to us as worshippers in the song, the entire emphasis is on the God we praise and worship. The heavenly worshipers continue with this song: "You are worthy, O Lord our God, to receive glory and honor and power. For you created all things, and they exist because you created what you pleased." (Rev. 4:11 NLT) Let's practice this kind of worship here and now!

In what practical ways can you worship the Lord better this year? _____

_____

_____

_____

_____

Church Martyr – Day 66

By Rob Hitt – International Board Member

Read Acts 7:54-60

BEYOND THE BORDERS ... According to Scripture, the first New Testament Church martyr was Stephen. Have you ever really focused on this account of his death and the implications there? After he proclaimed the Lord Jesus, he was taken outside and stoned to death. During his execution, before he left this world, he already saw into the Lord's presence. Scripture tells us that a saint's death, is "precious in the sight of the Lord'. We see the Lord welcoming Stephen into His presence and glory. But... what makes it more blessed is this; when Jesus ascended back to the Father after His resurrection, He SAT on the right hand of the Father. During Stephen's execution, he saw Jesus STANDING. We, as believers, are so loved by our Lord that Jesus stood when Stephen approached his final minutes. Standing when someone enters a room is a gesture of love and respect! WOW! How much the Lord really cares, loves and thinks about us! "Lord, thank you for caring and loving so much, when we are so undeserving. Amen."

Lying Lips – Day 67

By Craig Duck – President/Missionary FCFInternational

Read Proverbs 12:17-28

Encouragement for the day – *"Lying lips are an abomination to the LORD, But those who deal truthfully are His delight."*

Proverbs 12:22 NKJV

Firefighters love to tell stories, and some are better than others at it. Who doesn't love to sit around the station first thing in the morning, drinking coffee and talking about the "big one"? Sometimes, when I listen to stories I have to question within myself if the stories are true or not. Firefighters don't always tell the truth when it comes to storytelling. In fact, firefighters don't typically tell the truth when it comes to most things around the station. Not every firefighter lies, but a lot do. Whether it is to make themselves look better for promotion or election, or to have more friends, a lot of firefighters will lie.

The Bible encourages us to tell the truth in every situation. Christian firefighters need to set the standard around the station. We need to be known as people who can be counted on to always tell the truth, even if it hurts. According to proverbs God hates liars. If the Christian firefighter wants to please God we need to speak the truth. Speaking the truth is always easier said than done, but God promises to be with us, even at the station. The next time you feel like "stretching the truth" pray to God and ask for strength to tell the truth.

Lord, help me to be honest in every word that comes from my mouth.

Encouragement, pass it on!!

Notes

_____

_____

_____

_____

_____

_____

_____

_____

Thanks-living – Day 68

By Wayne Detzler – International Board Member

"Make thankfulness your sacrifice to God, and keep the vows you made to the Most High."

Psalm 50:14, 23 NLT

Thanksgiving is the key to a vibrant relationship with the Lord. During a particularly difficult time in our life of ministry, we visited a woman. She was incisive, and she had a pronounced gift of spiritual discernment. "When you pray," she advised, "frame the entire prayer in terms of thanksgiving." It turned my anxious spirit into a grateful spirit. Paul pursued this avenue of prayer, when he wrote to the Philippians: "Don't worry about anything; instead, pray about everything. Tell God what you need, and thank him for all he has done. Then you will experience God's peace, which exceeds anything we can understand. His peace will guard your hearts and minds as you live in Christ Jesus." (Phil. 4:6-7 NLT) So, turn thanksgiving into "thanks-living." It will change our whole outlook on life.

How has God blessed you in the past? _____

_____

_____

_____

Planting Seeds – Day 69

By Rob Hitt International Board Member

Encouragement for the day – *"Confess your trespasses[a] to one another, and pray for one another, that you may be healed. The effective, fervent prayer of a righteous man avails much."*

James 5:15 NKJV

The other day, I received a very nice email from the London Fire Brigade. Being a fire service history buff, I enjoyed scoping out their website and finding information on their history and the historical fires in London. I want to dedicate this article, to praying for the London Fire Brigade. May the Lord bless them and keep them in His care.

Whether firefighters are in our own local stations around the block or on the other side of the ocean, we need to remember to pray and encourage them in Jesus! The unique aspect of the fire service is that it provides a broad spectrum of ministry and outreach opportunities, both here and abroad. Prayerfully consider going on a fire service mission trip or sending FCFInternational materials to a distant fire department. One never knows what seeds may be planted, that will grow into an eternal reward!

Pushing Forward – Day 70

By Craig Duck – President/Missionary FCFInternational

Read Philippians 3:12-16

Encouragement for the day – *"I press toward the goal for the prize of the upward call of God in Christ Jesus."*

Philippians 3:14 NKJV

There are many philosophies in the fire service on how to extinguish fires. My dad told me of a time when they were taught to stick a hose line in the front window and whip it around. This would eventually create steam which in turn would put out the fire. That one didn't work so well. There has always been a debate on the use of a fog pattern verses a straight stream pattern. When I was a young firefighter I was taught to attack the fire from least burned and move to the most burned. Recently, the New York City Fire Department has been gathering scientific evidence to back the theory of hitting the fire quickly from the outside, knocking down visible fire, and then moving to the inside. One thing that worked for me over the years is setting the nozzle on straight stream, hitting the fire, and then pushing forward. I have always set the goal of extinguishing the fire, and I push forward until that goal is accomplished.

Paul encourages us in the book of Philippians to always press toward our goals in life. In Philippians, we are told to forget those things that are now in the past and to look forward to the things that are ahead. When we are fighting a fire our focus is always straight ahead at the fire that is still burning. We are not typically thinking of the fire we just extinguished, we are concentrating on what is still burning. In the Christian Firefighters life our goal should be for that upward calling that is found in Jesus Christ. As we live our life within the fire service community our lives should become more and more like Christ's. Paul knew when he wrote the book of Philippians that he still had some work to do in his life before he could obtain that goal. That is what drove Paul to write, "I press toward the goal". Are you pressing toward that goal today?

Lord, help me to always evaluate my life in light of how You want me to act.

Encouraging first responders to keep the faith!!

Notes

_____

_____

_____

Turning Outsiders into Insiders – Day 71

By Wayne Detzler – International Board Member

"What marvelous love the Father has extended to us! Just look at it—we're called children of God! That's who we really are. But that's also why the world doesn't recognize us or take us seriously, because it has no idea who he is or what he's up to."

1 John 3:1 The Message

God turns outsiders into insiders. He embraces us in His marvelous love. He welcomes us into His family. He makes us His own dear children—forever. One translation calls this, "lavish love." No words can describe the love of God, and He stands with open arms welcoming us into that love. Thank you Father for loving us!

How has God shown His great love to you in the past? ___

_____

What are some practical ways that you can show this love that God has for first responders to others in your department? _____

_____

_____

_____

Sufficient Grace – Day 72

By Craig Duck – President/Missionary FCFInternational

Read II Corinthians 12:7-10

Encouragement for the day – "And he said unto me, My grace is sufficient for thee: for my strength is made perfect in weakness. Most gladly therefore will I rather glory in my infirmities, that the power of Christ may rest upon me."

II Corinthians 12:9 KJV

I remember when I was a firefighter "running the line" for a busy engine company in Washington, DC. We tried our hardest to never rely on any other company other than our own. We had a truck company assigned to our station; however we enjoyed kicking down the doors before they arrived and utilizing our handline to ventilate when the fire was extinguished. We tried to be self-sufficient; however we soon realized that we needed help from other companies in order to consistently put fires out. We eventually had to admit that we were not always as strong as we wanted to be.

Paul reminds us that God's grace is sufficient for our walk with Him. God is all powerful and is strong, enough to handle anything in our lives that we struggle with. The trouble is we often feel like we can handle any situation through our own strength and we typically do not cry out to God until we are in too deep. It is far better for us to understand our weaknesses, admit this to God, and watch Him work through us. Then we truly see the "power of Christ" resting upon us. God's grace is all sufficient.

Lord, thank you that you are an all-powerful God who loves me.

Encouraging first responders to keep the faith!!

Notes

_____

_____

_____

_____

_____

_____

_____

_____

_____

Free Stuff – Day 73

By Keith Helms – International Board Member

We had the privilege of working at the FCFI booth in Indianapolis last week. As firefighters strolled past the booths, many of them were looking for the free stuff. Most attendees had bags stuffed full with the freebies. It was a true joy to tell firefighters about another free gift that they could receive. Our booth offered the gospel message of God's salvation through faith in Jesus Christ. We talked with firefighters about how they could have a personal relationship with Christ and how this relationship could grow through effective biblical discipleship. Many of our discussions were sparked by the firefighter sharing their struggles at home and at the station. Our desire was to encourage them to seek the Lord God; to study His word; and to allow the Holy Spirit to direct their hearts. Our free gift could not fit in the attendees bags. However our gift had the power to change men's hearts.

Do you want to know more about how your heart can be changed? Go to God's word and begin with these passages: Isaiah 55:1-2; Romans 6:23; John 3. Also, check out our website (fellowshipofchristianfirefighters.org) for Bible studies that will encourage you in your journey through a fallen, difficult world.

A Man of Prayer – Day 74

By Wayne Detzler – International Board Member

"Lord, teach us to pray," the disciples asked Jesus.

Luke 11:1 NLT

So, he gave them the pattern of prayer, the Lord's Prayer. The context shows how Jesus taught them to be prayer people. "And so I tell you, keep on asking, and you will receive what you ask for. Keep on seeking, and you will find. Keep on knocking, and the door will be opened to you. For everyone who asks, receives. Everyone who seeks, finds. And to everyone who knocks, the door will be opened." (Luke 11:9-10 NLT) The Lord is teaching us all to live lives of prayer, making prayer our first option and our constant practice. Ironically, I learned this practice from Billy Graham. As an occasional part of his team in Europe, I had a close view of a man of prayer. So, despite health and age issues, approaching his 95th birthday Mr. Graham is still a man of prayer.

Do you have a regular intimate time of prayer every day?

_____

If not, how can you make it a priority? _____

_____

112

Fully Equipped – Day 75

By Craig Duck – President/Missionary FCFInternational

Read II Timothy 3:10-17

Encouragement for the day – *"All Scripture is breathed out by God and profitable for teaching, for reproof, for correction, and for training in righteousness, that the man of God may be complete, equipped for every good work."*

II Timothy 3:16-17 ESV

We are spoiled in the fire service here in America. I just came back from a fire show from out on the west coast and I was able to walk around and look at all of the new fire trucks that the manufacturers are selling. They are filled with all sorts of firefighting equipment. Fire trucks have every type of couplings for connecting hose, tools for breaking apart things, ladders for getting into windows, and specialized equipment for all types of emergencies. I really enjoyed looking at all of the new equipment being offered to today's first responders. One of the manufacturers there was selling fire trucks "fully equipped", ready for immediate use.

I am thankful that God has not left us here to figure life out on our own. God has given us the Bible in order to help us get through life. We are told that the Bible is "God breathed", and is able to help the Christian firefighter with any circumstance that he or she comes across. The problem is not all Christian firefighters are reading and studying their Bibles. They may own one, but rarely do they pull it down from the shelf and read it. We don't buy a fire truck without equipment, leaving it parked in the station. Why then do we buy a Bible and leave it on the shelf. In II Timothy we learn that the Bible is profitable for all sorts of things for the Christian firefighter, we need to regularly read and study what it says. It is also profitable to memorize the Word of God in order to be prepared for life. How about you, are you fully equipped?

Lord, help me to read and study the Bible today that I might be fully equipped for life.

Encouragement, pass it on!!

Notes

_____

_____

_____

_____

_____

_____

_____

Engine Check Off – Day 76

By Rob Hitt – International Board Member

"Create in me a clean heart, O God, and renew a right spirit within me."

Psalm 51:10 ESV

BEYOND THE BORDERS ... Today on shift, one of our daily projects is engine check-offs and maintenance. This is done to insure that the apparatus is in working order when we need it in a critical moment. One of the daily checks is cleanliness. Washing/waxing the outside, says a lot to the general public plus it also keeps the engine in good condition for years of service ahead. One other factor to cleanliness is also cleaning the INSIDE. You probably know where this is going! We can look "clean" on the outside, but the Lord looks on the heart. John the Baptist addressed this issue when the Pharisees confronted Him. He stressed that they looked religious on the outside but were "full of dead men's bones". People can go to church, be baptized, "do good" and be a well-rounded person; but without Jesus, the inside is still dirty.

Lord, help us to evaluate and allow You to cleanse our hearts, in order for us to be more like You. Amen.

115

Children of the King – Day 77

By Wayne Detzler – International Board Member

Just reading the story of Elisha, and I came across one I had missed. A man brings the prophet a gift of bread and flour. Elisha uses the bread to feed one hundred people, and the Scripture commentary is: "And when they gave it to the people, there was plenty for all and some left over, just as the Lord had promised." (2 Kings 4:44 NLT) This reminds us of the feeding of the 5,000, when Jesus turned a little boy's lunch into a banquet for the crowd--and there were twelve full baskets left over. (John 6:1-13) Why is it? We often live like paupers when we are children of the King! The Lord can and will provide all our needs, "according to His riches in glory by Christ Jesus." (Phil. 4:19)

How has God blessed your life in the fire service? _____
_____

Has the Lord ever multiplied your blessings? _____
_____
_____
_____

Busy Night – Day 78

By Craig Duck President/Missionary FCFInternational

Read Matthew 11:25-29

Encouragement for the day – *"Come to Me, all you who labor and are heavy laden, and I will give you rest. Take My yoke upon you and learn from Me, for I am gentle and lowly in heart, and you will find rest for your souls."*

Matthew 11:28-29 NKJV

I slept in today at the firehouse. We had a busy night of responding to emergencies. Our company went on a couple of medical calls, an accident, and a box alarm for reported smoke on the third floor. It felt good to sleep in. I was tired from all of the activities and welcomed extra time to rest. Typically, I am up early at the firehouse in order to go home and tackle all of my jobs on the list I have.

Life can be busy for first responders. There are classes to take, online target safety courses to complete, and other important things to finish before the deadline. If you are a volunteer you have to do all of this on your own time after work. If you are a member of a local church there are activities that need to be attended as well as work around the church. Those with families have all sorts of activities they must go back and forth to. Life for today's firefighters can be extremely busy and stressful for even the strongest of Christian Firefighters. Occasionally it is good to get away and rest for a while. The Bible encourages us to come to Jesus and He will give us rest for our souls. So I recommend that you take a day off every now and then. Spend a relaxing day with your spouse, take the family somewhere that doesn't take effort but is fun, or spend time relaxing around the house reading the Word of God. Whatever you decide to do, take some time and rest.

Lord, help me to find my rest in You.

Encouraging the fire service, one first responder at a time!!

Notes

_____

_____

_____

_____

_____

_____

_____

Dark Days – Day 79

By Wayne Detzler – International Board Member

"How long must I take counsel in my soul and have sorrow in my heart all the day?"

Psalm 13:2 NLT

Even David had bad days. He faced tough enemies and family crises. In these "dark nights of the soul," David felt as if God was not hearing his prayers. Sometimes the pressures of life threaten to crush the life out of us. Then we make a discovery like David did. He finishes this little psalm with this ringing affirmation: "But I have trusted in your steadfast love; my heart shall rejoice in your salvation." (Psalm 13:5 NLT)

What difficulties have you gone through in the past year?

_____

_____

What Bible verses helped you to go through those difficult days? _____

_____

_____

First Due – Day 80

By Craig Duck – President/Missionary FCFInternational

Read I Thessalonians 4:9-18

Encouragement for the day – *"For the Lord himself shall descend from heaven with a shout, with the voice of the archangel, and with the trump of God: and the dead in Christ shall rise first:"*

I Thessalonians 4:16 KJV

In Washington, DC the words that every firefighter loves to hear is "First Due". When a box alarm is sounded for a reported fire, communications will list the companies due on the box alarm in order of their assignment. The company that is first due is responsible for finding a hydrant close to the building, stretching their attack line into the building, and extinguishing the fire. Firefighters love to put the fires out that they go to, and being first due is the best chance of accomplishing that goal. When a box alarm is sounded and a company has been placed first due, those firefighters assigned to that position typically get more excited than the rest of the box. All of the companies will end up at the box, however only one company can be first due.

120

In I Thessalonians we read about a day when those who have trusted in Jesus Christ as their Lord and Savior will get to go to heaven. Paul in this passage of the Bible is talking about the end of the world. In that day, Paul explains, that there is an order of arrival. This order is similar to that of our dispatch system. In fact, the very call of God is similar to how we dispatch box alarms. Before a box alarm is dispatched two long tones precede the dispatch of companies. At the end of the world there will be the sound of the trump of God. This sound will be heard throughout the whole world. Then the dispatch will occur. What's the order you say? "The dead in Christ will rise first", then "we who are alive and remain shall be caught up together with them in the clouds". Then we will be "on scene", and will be with the Lord forever.

Lord, thank you that Jesus Christ has paid the ultimate price that I may have access to heaven.

Encouragement, now that is real comforting!!

Notes

_____

_____

_____

_____

Faith is the Victory – Day 81

By Wayne Detzler – International Board Member

"Faith is the victory that overcomes the world," I woke up singing in my heart this old song. It is amazing, but God always comes through with just the encouragement that is needed. As we launch into a new week at the university and in online teaching, the pace becomes faster, more intense. Students are surging to finish the work before the 8-week online courses end, and this ups the workload for the professor. At the same time teaching intensifies at our church, and the publisher's deadline for my book looms nearer. Pressure is one of the levers Satan uses to stress us out. But the truth of Scripture remains: "For everyone who has been born of God overcomes the world. And this is the victory that has overcome the world—our faith." (1 John 5:4 ESV)

What pressures do you face in your department that might take your focus of the Lord? _____

_____

_____

_____

Graduation Day – Day 82

By Craig Duck – President/Missionary FCFInternational

Read Philippians 1:1-11

Encouragement for the day *"Being confident of this very thing, that He who began a good work in you will complete it until the day of Jesus Christ."*

Philippians 1:6 NKJV

When I was first hired in the District of Columbia Fire and EMS Department I went right into recruit school at the training academy. The academy training was some of the toughest fire training I had ever received. I had been a volunteer firefighter before and went through a lot of classes, but nothing compared to my experience in Washington. I was up late at night studying and up early in the morning to go to school. The days were long as they were filled with both physical and mental learning. I will never forget how much the instructors cared for us, working hard to ensure that we graduated.

The Christian walk is very similar to that training academy experience. As you walk through life with God you will quickly discover that it can be hard. That is why Jesus said; "in the world you will have tribulation; but be of good cheer, I have overcome the world" (Matthew 16:33

NKJV). Sometimes the trials can be so severe that it will take sheer determination and a spirit that fully relies on God for strength. During those times it is comforting to know that God will not abandon us. God will never say "I didn't see that one coming". God is in control of not only our lives, but of the entire universe. God started something very special in you and He will complete that work.

Lord, it is easy to get discouraged in life. Help me to fully rely on you today and always.

Encouragement, something we all should be doing!!

Notes

_____

_____

_____

_____

_____

_____

_____

_____

_____

Walking in Blindness Day 83

By Keith Helms – International Board Member

Read John Chapter 3

The physically blind person walks in darkness, but it is not by choice. The proud person also walks in darkness; however his blindness is a chosen path. He does not want to know the true condition of his heart. Exposure of his heart would uncover his inability to create a world that validates his desire for importance and control. So, the proud person prefers to avoid the deepest issues of the heart. Like the Pharisees in Matthew 23, he proudly parades his religious acts, convinced that he is spiritually mature. However, his true condition is one of self-deception. Jeremiah 17:9 states that the heart is deceitfully wicked. The proud person does not want to open his heart to the light; he chooses to walk in darkness (John 3:19-20). His motto could be "out of sight…out of mind." As long as he refuses to acknowledge his heart's true condition based on God's light, he can tell himself (and others) that he is managing life well.

The broken person wants to walk in the light. He wants God's light to be cast on his heart. In Jeremiah 17:10 we are told that although the heart is deceitfully wicked, God searches the heart and tests the mind. His light will expose our deeds of the flesh, providing the opportunity for brokenness and repentance. The broken person looks at this as a continuous, never ceasing process. He seeks to "walk in the light", not stop by the light for a momentary spiritual examination. It is not a periodic check on his spiritual status. By walking in the light, the broken person has a constant check on his status. He knows how easily he can be deceived by the flesh. By walking in the light and depending on the Spirit, the broken person can walk a path that is honoring and glorifying to the Lord.

Notes

_____

_____

_____

_____

_____

_____

_____

_____

Every Knee will Bow – Day 84

By Wayne Detzler – International Board Member

"Jesus, Jesus, Jesus,

there's just something about that Name.

Master, Savior, Jesus,

like the fragrance after the rain.

Jesus, Jesus, Jesus,

let all heaven and earth proclaim.

Kings and kingdoms will all pass away.

But there's something about that Name."

(Bill and Gloria Gaither)

Early this morning I woke with these words ringing in my heart. There is nothing more comforting, nothing more encouraging than the name of Jesus. "At the Name of Jesus every knee will bow, in heaven, and on earth, and under the earth, and every tongue confess that Jesus is Lord to the glory of God the Father." (Phil. 2:9-11)

In what practical ways can you give thanks to God for what He has done for you and proclaim His wonderful name to others in the fire service? _____

_____

_____

_____

Leadership – Day 85

By Craig Duck – President/Missionary FCFInternational

Read Mark 10:35-45

Encouragement for the day – *"and whoever wants to be first must be slave of all. For even the Son of Man did not come to be served, but to serve, and to give his life as a ransom for many."*

Mark 10:44-45 NIV

The fire service is filled with various types of leaders with all sorts of ideas on how to lead. There are the leaders who want to be everyone's friend. These types of leaders love to hang out with everyone, trying to be well liked. Typically these types of leaders will never accomplish much but will have lots of friends. On the opposite side of the fence is the authoritarian leader. They love to rule with an iron fist and bark out orders in order to get things done. It is their way or the highway and don't even suggest a better way to do it. Every type of leadership style written in books can be found in the fire service.

The Bible has the best leadership plan available and it comes with an example that worked. Jesus taught his disciples that the mark of a true leader is one who serves others. Jesus said; "whoever desires to be great among you shall be your servant". As a Christian firefighter we should have a humble servant attitude as a leader, no matter what our rank is. Some of the greatest officers I know help out with clean up around the firehouse, shovel snow off the sidewalks, and do more than the required holding of the radio at a fire. When we as officers begin to humble ourselves and serve those who work with us we will become an effective godly leader and show a lost fire service the love of Jesus.

Lord, help me to be a godly leader at the firehouse you have called me to.

Encouragement should be everybody's assignment for the day!!

Notes

_____

_____

_____

_____

_____

_____

_____

Giving Like Jesus – Day 86

By Wayne Detzler – International Board Member

"I tell you the truth," Jesus said, "this poor widow has given more than all the rest of them. For they have given a tiny part of their surplus, but she, poor as she is, has given everything she has."

Luke 21:3-4 NLT

As usual, Jesus turns our reasoning on its head. We admire wealthy people who give much to God's work. I have wished for a long time I could endow a professorial chair in missions—just a dream. We look at the outside, but Jesus looks at our hearts. He knew that the widow had given all she had—her motives were pure. At Black Rock Church we are learning how to give like Jesus, and this Bible passage gives valuable insight.

Do you regularly give out of the abundance of what the Lord has blessed you with? _____

How can we give to further the kingdom of God in the fire service? _____

_____

_____

Never Give Up – Day 87

By Craig Duck – President/Missionary FCFInternational

Read I Thessalonians 3

"But as for you brethren, do not grow weary in doing good"

II Thessalonians 3:13 NKJV

I love the fire service. I am so thankful to God that He has allowed me to serve in such a great field as ours. One thing I love is how first responders always get things done. Think back on all the emergency calls our great nation has had this year. No matter how big the emergency is, firefighters always rise to the occasion and get things done. This past year there has been some big emergencies that firefighters have been called to; wildfires in the west, tornadoes, floods, hurricanes, and big fires. If you were there you would have seen the faces of tired men and women who gave their all in order to bring the chaos back to a sense of normal. First responders never give up.

Today's Bible verse encourages believers in Christ to have the same attitude as Christian first responders. We all know there is evil in the world and sometimes it feels like that evil is directed toward us. The deceiver would like nothing better than for Christian Firefighters to give up.

When we quit, chaos wins. Just like a wildfire where firefighters give up and the fire gets bigger. So is the fire service doomed to get worse if believers give up and stop doing "good". The next time you feel like giving up because of difficulty or lack of participation, remember that God wants us to keep going. I challenge you today to do one good thing for someone at your local station that does not know Jesus Christ as their personal Savior. Let them know how much Jesus loves them.

Lord, give me the strength to keep going even if nobody is following.

Encouragement, share it with a friend!!

Notes

_____

_____

_____

_____

_____

_____

_____

_____

Glory – Day 88

By Wayne Detzler – International Board Member

"Worship the Lord in the splendor of his holiness."

Psalm 29:2 NLT

This psalm combines the glory of God's creation with the glory of worship. It reaches its peak in the phrase, "In his Temple everyone shouts, 'Glory!'" (Psalm 29:9 NLT) Yesterday I drove past the construction site of our dear Black Rock Church. The shape of a large worship center is emerging, sculptured in steel. Arches of the old church stand as a welcome corridor leading to the vast new church. In the corner of the steel skeleton is a small room that will be our prayer room. We are so blessed to be part of the prayer ministry as we look forward to the day, when everyone will shout, "Glory!" We will worship God in the splendor of His great holiness in our new worship center.

How do you typically praise God? _____

_____

_____

What Survives the Fire – Day 89

By Keith Helms – International Board Member

"For we must all appear before the judgment seat of Christ, so that each of us may receive what is due us for the things done while in the body, whether good or bad."

II Corinthians 5:10 NIV

I was always amazed at what would remain after a fully involved structure fire. Many valuable items survived because they were hidden from the damaging heat. A good example would be a family Bible. The cover would often be damaged beyond repair, but you could open the book and clearly read the words. Furthermore, I once saw a dog run out of a house that was a total loss, about 15 minutes after the control time. I have no idea how he survived the fire.

A day is coming when every believer will experience a fire. It will be a fire of judgment. The Bible calls it The Judgment Seat of Christ. This judgment is not to determine whether a person is going to heaven or hell. It is to examine everything that a believer did in this life. The standard is very high. Not only will our works be tested, our motives will be examined (1 Cor. 4:5). The things that we did for God's glory will survive the heat and will be rewarded. The things that are determined to be for our own glory will be consumed by the fire. Many good works will be reduced to ashes because the motives of the heart were opposed to God and His glory. The question for each of us is what have I done today that will be rewarded after the Judgment Seat of Christ? What have I done that reflects the image of Christ? Never forget that the primary issue is the motives of your heart. Ask the Holy Spirit to help you to clearly see your motives (Psalm 139:23-24). Pray that your motives will be pure, escaping the coming fire. The rewards will endure for eternity.

What are you currently doing that glorifies God in the fire service? _____

_____

_____

How can we test our motives for the things we do? _____

_____

_____

In what ways can you encourage others in your department to glorify God in the fire service? _____

_____

_____

Safety Officer – Day 90

By Craig Duck – President/Missionary FCFInternational

Read Proverbs 16:10-19

Encouragement for the day – *"The highway of the upright avoids evil; the one who guards his way protects his life"*
Proverbs 16:17 Holman Christian Standard

The fire service has introduced the safety officer to the ranks of most departments. In the District of Columbia Fire and EMS Department we have one safety officer per shift, and that person is a captain. The job of the safety officer is to ensure that firefighters do their job as safe as possible. Safety officers will test new gear and equipment, investigate incidents where firefighters get injured, and ensure that operations on the fireground are safe for firefighters. All of this effort is to ensure that firefighters don't get hurt and can efficiently handle emergencies that they are called to.

The Bible acts as our safety officer. Throughout its pages the Bible has proven truths that will keep us from harm. It's not that God wants to be mean spirited and have a whole bunch of rules to make us discouraged. God wants us to avoid things and circumstances that will hurt us and cause us pain. God does this because of His great love for us. Today's verse encourages us to avoid evil. There are firefighters that want you as a Christian firefighter to fall and commit sin. If you know that firefighters are going to do something that is wrong and goes against what the Bible says, Proverbs warns you to avoid it. When Christian firefighters avoid evil they will be safe, protecting their very life.

Lord, help me today to avoid evil by following the truths contained in the Bible.

Encouragement, pass it on!!

Notes

_____

_____

_____

_____

_____

_____

_____

_____

_____

FCFInternational

Mission Statement – To glorify God in the fire service by building relationships that turn first responders heart and minds toward Christ (Philippian 2:11), equipping them to serve Him (Ephesians 4:12)

Vision Statement – To encourage one another to share the vision with the fire service through **W**itnessing, **P**raying, **T**eaching the Word, **W**alking worthy.

Contact Information
International Office
249 Rochichi Drive
Boydton, VA 23917
443-336-9859
fcfihq@aol.com

www.fellowshipofchristianfirefighters.org